F*CK

Stefanie Sword–Williams

BEING
HUMBLE

Why Self-Promotion Isn't a Dirty Word

Hardie Grant

QUADRILLE

Publishing Director Sarah Lavelle
Commissioning Editor Susannah Otter
Assistant Editor Stacey Cleworth
Art Director and Designer Luke Bird
Typesetter Jonathan Baker
Head of Production Stephen Lang
Production Controller Sinead Hering

Published in 2020 by Quadrille,
an imprint of Hardie Grant Publishing

Quadrille
52–54 Southwark Street
London SE1 1UN
quadrille.com

Cataloguing in Publication Data: a catalogue record
for this book is available from the British Library.
Text © Stefanie Sword-Williams, 2020
Design and layout © Quadrille 2020

ISBN 978 1 78713 513 0
Printed in Italy

FSC
www.fsc.org
MIX
Paper from
responsible sources
FSC® C115118

To my family for empowering me with limitless self-belief, my friends and boyfriend for continuous unconditional support, and to anyone who has ever supported the platform with an open mind and appetite to grow.

I couldn't have done it without you all.

CONTENTS

INTRODUCTION   6

1. SELF-PROMOTION IS NOT A DIRTY WORD   10
(it's the defining factor of your success)

2. KNOWING WHAT YOU STAND FOR   30
(working out what you want and crafting your profile towards it)

3. DON'T BE IN HIDING   52
(make sure you're present in all the right places)

4. THE POWER OF NETWORKING   68
(and why it's a game-changer when growing your career)

5. KNOWING YOUR SELF-WORTH 104

(how to recognise and demonstrate what you bring to the table)

6. GETTING THE MONEY YOU WANT 130

(how to get what you deserve)

7. CALM THE F*CK DOWN 152

(why emotional intelligence is the secret component)

8. FAILURES MAKE YOU FUNNY 202

(we all do it, here's how to handle it when it happens)

9. DON'T LET LABELS LIMIT YOU 218

(keep striving until you find what makes you truly happy)

READING LIST 224

INTRODUCTION

'F*CK BEING HUMBLE'

Not a saying you hear a lot, is it?

Of course not. Until this very moment, you've spent your entire life being told that being humble is how you earn respect; and, while there is merit in the sentiment, trust me when I say it's not quite that straightforward. You see, you can be the humblest person in the world, but if you're not willing to be your own champion, you might be waiting a long while for someone to bow down and kiss those Stan Smiths of yours.

Sadly, we live in a world where the word 'self-promotion' has acquired so many negative connotations that being associated with it is as embarrassing as getting a tattoo on your arse in Magaluf. Yuck. But what is it about putting ourselves out there that we're really scared of?

An acronym I've coined to summarise the paralysis we face is FOSS (Fear Of Sounding Stupid). This is the anxiety that the very way you describe yourself could be classed as cringeworthy or self-indulgent – or worse still, could be challenged for not reflecting who you really are. But while you're busy obsessing over how the rest of the world perceives you (by the way, everyone else is doing exactly the same thing and isn't thinking about you anyway), the real problem you should be facing is FOBG (Fear Of Being Generic). Now, I know that doesn't roll off the tongue quite as well as FOSS, but just stick with me ...

FOBG is what should really be keeping you up at night, because you, my friend, are most likely doing everything you possibly can to *not* stand out – and you may not even realise it. You follow the rules, you communicate the way you think is expected of you, you're modest, and you definitely don't send a weekly roundup of your latest work. Instead, you sit in 'Camp Generic' with your Nando's medium chicken and piri-piri salted chips.

Don't worry – it's normal; we all do it. In fact, it's *too* normal. There are many things that may be stopping you from self-promotion: concerns around sounding arrogant; a severe lack of confidence; and the one that suffocates people the most ... you don't know where to start and you feel too embarrassed to ask. But let me ask you a question: were you born a talking, cycling, cartwheeling adult? No, you were taught all of those things throughout childhood, or even as an adult.

The truth is, we have never been trained in self-promotion, a skill that is integral to building a career, whatever your industry. Whether you're in full-time employment, working as a freelancer or running your own business, failing to master this one skill can lead you down the common path towards a quarter or mid-life crisis of feeling undervalued, lost, and dissatisfied with where your career is going.

So why now? What is it about the world we live in that means we have to start taking this a whole lot more seriously? Well, the recession has meant job security is a dying breed, and our rising expectations of flexibility and freedom mean we need to find a way to not only stand on our own two feet, but rise above everyone else who's developing side hustles on their lunch breaks. With freelancers accounting for 77 million people globally and younger people wanting to become their own bosses sooner (the number of self-employed workers aged 16 to 24 has nearly doubled since 2001), the question is: Are we equipped to take on the real world?

Our education has been focused on endowing us with knowledge, but not necessarily the soft skills we need to make it in our careers. According to LinkedIn's 2019 *Global Talent Trends* report, with automation and AI reshaping the future of the workplace, it's the personal attributes you can bring to a business that companies are looking at when recruiting: '82% of UK employers said that finding individuals with soft skills was more important than hiring those with "hard" skills such as a programming language with a limited shelf life.'

The gig economy may be growing, but unless your confidence in tackling self-promotion and asking for your worth is too, I'd wave goodbye to any thoughts you've had about building a thriving business or remotely working on a beach in South America. From not regularly updating your platforms to shying away from asking for referrals or sharing personal work, there is still a significant disconnect between the lives we want to lead and our ability to build and maintain them. We expect the pay rises, the recognition and the belief from others, but we don't give people enough reason to provide them ... and then we complain when all our stars don't perfectly align.

The good news is, you're reading this book because you've finally recognised the importance of sorting your shit out if you want to get far in life.

I have spent the past seven years working in advertising producing stories for brands all over the world, and I think it is with that knowledge and exposure of seeing the positive impact storytelling can have for brands that I have realised the positive impact it can have on individuals too. But I also recognise that not everyone is sitting on the frontline of 'Mad Men' style meetings to see the significance of promotion, particularly if you're not working in the creative industry. How would you ever learn how to piece your personal brand together, let alone figure out how to shout about it. It was with this observation that I saw a huge gap in support that 'F*ck Being Humble' can fill. Learning how to self-promote shouldn't just be for TV hosts, or musicians, or artists, it should be accessible for people in every industry, worldwide. Since launching the platform I have delivered workshops to a variety of brands such as Unilever, The British Red Cross, Google, Warner Music, Smartworks, Bumble, General Assembly and many more, highlighting that the demands for alternative professional development practices are high across a variety of sectors.

The beautiful thing about the sharing economy lifestyle that we're in means that it's not just houses and cars we're sharing, peer-to-peer coaching is becoming more accessible too. As Sapphire Bates from the Coven Girl Gang – an online community of female founders and freelancers – would say, we're the 'community over competition' generation. (Hell yes to that.) The old-school idea of what makes a role model is fading out, and new icons like Gina Martin, Jameela Jamil, Malala Yousafzai and Toni Harris are rolling in. I could have waited for my career to pan out and write this book in 20 years, but this problem needs solving – and it needs solving fast. Your incredible talents shouldn't slip through the cracks just because you haven't been taught how to make them visible to the world.

There is a way to self-promote with integrity; I'm going to show you how.

ONE

SELF-PROMOTION IS NOT A DIRTY WORD

hen I started off on this journey and told people that my goal was to help people overcome their fears of self-promotion, I was met with pretty universal looks of disapproval. These only deepened when I explained that the platform was called 'F*ck Being Humble'. Even *I* used to lower my voice, just in case it offended people. (I know, believe in your brand and all that, but you can't help feeling nervous saying such a provocative phrase to a 60-year-old businessman.)

The funny thing is, it's the provocative title that has connected with people the most – it cuts through the stuffy and rigid status quo of career development and strikes a chord with people of all ages. But while I became more confident openly sharing the brand, and momentum built around the movement, certain people's responses still didn't change.

For some, the concern stemmed from not being able to accept that self-promotion is a skill that is essential in modern business; but for most people, it was simply that they had no idea what the term really meant. Self-promotion for Brits, in particular, is almost taboo, and it is very rarely encouraged through our education system or during our careers. Which, of course, I would argue is absolutely ridiculous. We tiptoe around a topic that can make all the difference in being paid appropriately, or finding a fulfilling career, or making meaningful connections in the workplace, and yet we're force-fed geometry from the age of 11 – and, quite frankly, I don't know when I've ever needed to know whether an angle is acute or obtuse.

The concerns around 'blowing your own trumpet' overshadow the benefits of self-promotion. Somewhere along the way the definition has got lost – and, consequently, people avoid it like they avoid being sandwiched between sweaty commuters on the tube at 9 a.m. Because, when you actually break it down, 'self' means *I* and 'promotion' means *an activity that supports or encourages a cause, venture, or aim*. So my regular response to the raised eyebrows and cynical attitude is: What's arrogant about that? How can you possibly dismiss it as self-indulgent or say 'it's just not for me', when really you've probably already engaged with that 'activity' at some point in your life – you just never openly labelled it as 'self-promotion' and nor have you thought about how you could be doing it better?

You're most likely reading this book because, deep down, you *do* want to share with the world how good you really are, but you don't know how to do it in a way that won't invite people to judge you. Because, ultimately, no matter how proud you are of your work, the fear of sharing it – and how you'll be perceived when you do – is what you care about most. Your lack of knowledge on how to put your talents out there effectively creates an irrational fear that you will be ripped to shreds or even dismissed for oversharing – which is ironic, as I bet it doesn't stop you from sharing Instagram stories of you shrieking karaoke at 5 a.m. with all your mates.

But we'll breeze past that and look at why society has set us up to fail. It's much easier to blame everyone else, isn't it?

MODESTY IS NOT ALWAYS THE ANSWER

Throughout your life, you will have most likely been encouraged to always, *always* be modest about your achievements. And despite what the title of this book might suggest, I do believe in humility, 100 per cent. What I don't agree with is letting yourself be so humble that you miss the opportunity of a lifetime, all because you're 'far too modest'. No one will pat you on the back for that. In fact, when you're starting out in your career, you must work 10 times harder to get noticed, because you haven't earned a reputation that will allow you to sit back and lap up the praise. When no one knows who you are, it's really more arrogant – as well as naive – to trust that everything will land in your lap if you wait patiently. Because it won't. But you're not solely to blame for this humble pie approach – society is too. So let's look at who and what may have impacted the way you self-promote ...

YOUR PARENTS

Most parents didn't want their child to be a cocky, snot-faced brat that no one likes, so bragging about your achievements was likely a no-go unless it was to your grandma and grandad, who already worshipped the ground you walked on. Chances are they also work in a completely different industry to you, and so their career advice, although given with love, probably isn't right for you and your journey, particularly when you think about the ways in which our professional trajectories have changed. We are more likely to freelance outside of our day jobs, we generate business via Twitter, we can work remotely from anywhere in the world, and some of us are even building empires from our bedrooms at the age of 13.

We also have less job security than our parents did. Mark Lurie, founder and CEO at Codex Protocol, explains that our parents were used to working hard for a company in exchange for a long-term investment in skills development and future financial security, like a retirement fund or pension. But employment security and long-term investment no longer exist in the modern working world. Over the last 20 years, the number of companies the average individual works for in the five years after they graduate has nearly doubled. We can't trust that we'll be in the same industry – let alone company – for our whole career, and that has had a huge impact on the way we work.

YOUR EDUCATION

Education is meant to prep you for the world ahead of you, and while I understand that no course can cover every topic, there is very often little time spent on knowing what you stand for and how to effectively communicate your achievements. At school, you're usually met with an unenthusiastic careers advisor and then left to write a personal statement by yourself with minimal coaching (which, from memory, was soul-destroying). Stephen Guise, author of *Mini Habits: Smaller Habits, Bigger Results*, summarises it perfectly: 'Instead of learning critical life skills on how to manage money, how to negotiate, or how to communicate, kids are mostly taught to memorise information. This is helpful to learn, but not at the cost of not learning critical life skills.' And it doesn't get much better throughout your degree – you're so focused on passing exams and submitting a dissertation, securing that dream role at the same time feels completely unachievable. Particularly when the advice on differentiating yourself once you graduate, writing killer CVs and prepping for interviews is not part of the curriculum. Is it any surprise that Universities UK found that one in three graduates ends up being 'mismatched' to the job they find after leaving education?

YOUR BOSS

Your superiors are (sadly) not your hype men. It's very rare to find a selfless, self-confident boss who wants to champion you and all your goodness to the rest of the business. Of course, some of them are terrified you'll overtake them, but for most managers and employers, it's simply the fact that they're more focused on achieving their own goals than shouting about how great you are. In Deloitte's 2018 Global Human Capital Trends survey, 58 per cent of respondents rated their organisations as 'not effective' or 'only somewhat effective' at empowering people to manage their own careers.

As a result, the lack of a proper employee development plan becomes the leading cause of losing young talent. The creative industries in particular struggle with this problem. Despite making unbelievably cool stuff all the time, you're rarely encouraged to share your work – at the risk of it looking too 'braggy'. Instead, you wait and silently hope that the CEO will eventually spot your talent (six years later) and reward you accordingly.

THE MEDIA

We've all watched a thousand films and read countless clickbaity articles built on the idea of dreams coming true when someone stumbles into their big break. What's covered less frequently is just how hard people work to become an 'overnight' success. We're sold the idea of being one in a million, but it's more likely that you're just one of a million people vying for the same opportunities. Unfortunately, popular culture has set us up to believe that if our talent isn't 'spotted' – if we don't naturally stand out from the crowd without any conscious effort on our part – then we don't really have any talent at all. We see Kris Jenner, the world's most famous momager, making dreams happen for her daughters and view it as something normal; but, in reality, no one makes it to the Victoria's Secret catwalk or becomes the 'youngest Forbes self-made billionaire' without some serious work behind the scenes.

YOUR SURROUNDING ENVIRONMENT

There's no denying that the cultural environment that surrounds you will have affected your feelings about self-promotion and your ability to give it a try. Americans, for example, are famously willing and able to talk about themselves and their achievements. It's like they have a secret handbook that teaches you to communicate just how bloody brilliant you are. So much so that, in the 1980s, California politician John Vasconcellos set up a state task force to promote high self-esteem as the answer to all social ills. While it may not have solved homelessness and violence as he hoped, it definitely demonstrated a belief in self-promotion that other parts of the world just don't have.

It's not just where you were raised – attitudes to self-promotion can be affected by religious and cultural factors, too. Nafisa Bakkar, founder of Amaliah.com, an insights and media platform for Muslim women, explains that, within the Islamic faith, there is the belief that everything comes from God's plan and so self-promotion and sharing personal achievements should be grounded in the knowledge that it was possible because of God, rather than individual efforts alone.

For black people, it is the cultural and systemic barriers in the society we live in that create challenges for understanding how to navigate self-promotion. In the book *Slay in Your Lane*, the inspirational guide to life for a generation of black British women, co-author Elizabeth Uviebinené explains, 'When you're anything other than the default white male, there is always going to be something that's uniquely different about your experiences. Being black women, there are so many issues that you have to be aware of when you enter spaces that are not set up for you.' Being seen and not heard is something black women suffer the worst from as they are often made to feel lucky to have a seat at the table at all.

Additionally, for many black British women, being told to work twice as hard to get half as much as their white counterparts is normalised as a life lesson to the working world. Elizabeth also goes on to explain in the book that her parents would 'steer them to careers such as law and medicine, professions in which no one could deny qualifications, regardless of the colour of your skin and the prejudice you might come across.' When whiteness is the norm and everyone else is othered, it is this lived experience of structural inequality that leaves a regular feeling of coming second place, affecting both confidence and self-belief, which consequently affects the outlook on self-promotion.

YOUR GENDER

Of course, we can't ignore the fact that, although we've seen dramatic progress in gender equality over the past 10 years, the gender pay gap, the proportion of senior positions occupied by females and the acceptance of women pursuing certain careers is still an issue globally. For every female empowerment campaign urging us to follow our dreams, there is still a case of public shaming – like Jim Carrey commenting that Margot Robbie's success is a result of her good looks as opposed to her talent – that further cements a culture in which women's successes aren't celebrated the same as men's. As a result, we see that women are more susceptible to imposter syndrome (the feeling of not having earned the right to your success), which, according to a 2018 Access Commercial Finance study, affects two-thirds of women at work in the UK. Gender bias has deprived and continues to deprive females of opportunities, starting in childhood and extending throughout our working lives. To all the men struggling with self-promotion too, I hear you and see you, but it is important to acknowledge the additional limitations that women face.

The surroundings in which we're raised are intrinsically linked to how we communicate ourselves. Of course, you can spend your life blaming society for not preparing you (which is what we like to do for most shortcomings), or you can accept that being encouraged to be humble does have its perks. You're unlikely to be a pain to be around, most people probably like you, and you're yet to be accused of being self-obsessed – but that can only take you so far. The way I explain it is, you can sit patiently waiting for the opportunities to come to you, or you can go out and chase them yourself. There will always be a place for modesty in your career, but you can't let it overtake the hustle.

IT'S ALL IN YOUR MIND

When I hear the words 'self-promotion isn't for me', I cry a little inside. Outside of the (often misleading) influences we've just explored, you've most likely come to that conclusion based on either a lack of knowledge as to *how* to self-promote, or a lack of confidence that limits your ability to share. Both of these things can be changed – if you're willing to change them yourself. But first, let's get some things clear. When I say 'self-promotion', I don't mean standing on your office chair shouting about just how great your latest piece of work is. I mean *being prepared*. Being prepared for someone to google you, for an impromptu meeting, for opportunities that have the ability to shape your future before you've even had time to realise it. It's about embracing the benefits of a world that is 'always on' without having to be 'always on' yourself.

We live in a hyper-connected world, and of course there are some undeniable highs and lows that come with that. The highs are that, at the click of a button, I can be 'connected' with the CEO of Patagonia on the other side of the world; or I can start a movement from the comfort of my own living room while watching *Love Island* with my mates. You've got to admit, it's pretty incredible that technology has broken down so many barriers for us. But our career-obsessed culture means that we can be our own worst enemies when it comes to the pressure and expectations we put on ourselves. In fact, according to LinkedIn, 75 per cent of 25- to 33-year-olds have experienced a quarter-life crisis, with the top reasons for anxiety being 'finding a job or career they're passionate about' and 'comparing themselves to their more successful friends'. This, I'm sure, you can empathise with.

The real shame of it all is that it's forced us to waste so much time and energy lusting after things that aren't actually important to us. Envying Insta-bloggers for getting loads of free stuff, even though you know that girl with 500k followers is sat in a restaurant with someone who isn't actually her friend taking those 700 'candid' photos. Or feeling the pressure to be a 'female self-made entrepreneur' because the #girlboss slogan has made it onto your makeup bag, even though you've never actually had a desire to become a business owner. We benchmark our personal success against the successes of others every day, which just isn't healthy: not for our mind, our ambitions or our enjoyment of life.

If it makes you feel any better, it's not a new thing. 'Social comparison theory' was identified back in the 1950s – it's just become more apparent now because of our seemingly unbreakable relationship with social media. According to the man behind the theory, Leon Festinger, when people are incapable of evaluating their own opinions and abilities, they tend to compare themselves with others. It often starts with unreasonable comparisons to others who have achieved at unusually high levels – which, unsurprisingly, leads you to boarding the never-ending anxiety train, worrying about your own progress in life. Sound familiar? Of course it does – we've all been there (or maybe still are?).

Festinger pointed out two things that are crucial for an individual's own suc-cess. First, comparing your own achievements to those of your peers will make you miserable; and second, if you *must* compare yourself to someone, don't choose the really bloody successful people, because you'll just end up feeling utterly worthless. It's common sense really, but it's so easy to get swept up in a WhatsApp group of envy where it feels like everyone is succeeding except you. If it's not being jealous of your actual mates, it's coveting the look of a rising fitness influencer who obtained those abs via a personal trainer seven days a week and relentless healthy eating.

So how do you overcome this crippling sense of inadequacy? You be real with yourself, by knowing what you actually want and preparing for it at whatever pace feels right for you. It's okay not to be a CEO at 24. A quick reality check: before the age of 40, Samuel L. Jackson hadn't yet had a major role in a movie, Judge Judy hadn't made it onto daytime TV and Vera Wang hadn't designed her first wedding dress. You might even figure out what you want but not reach the dream for another 50 years, because everyone 'makes it' at different points in their lives. That's just the way it is. Stop putting the pressure on yourself to be an almighty success machine, and focus on your own victories – however big or small they might be.

THE (LACK OF) CONFIDENCE CYCLE

The word 'confidence' is something we have to discuss, because it truly is the driver of your success, and sadly it can be so easily knocked at any stage of your life for so many reasons: a shitty boss, a toxic relationship, weight issues – or, the killer, that you just don't think you're good enough at your job.

I've identified three barriers to feeling confident in yourself and your work. Any one of these (or all of them) could be what's holding you – and your ability to self-promote – back ...

1. CLASS A CLINGING

You may have heard this phrase as a way to describe a slightly needy girl or guy who starts planning your wedding after the first date; however, I'm talking about the *career* 'class A clingers' here. You'll know them well, and may even spot yourself in this description ...

You continue to stay with a company even though you know your boss is a wanker, your company is completely fixed in its ways and you struggle to find the inspiration to go to work every day. You've spent enough time there by now to feel completely underrated and are watching newbies come in and rise above you while you sit questioning why you've still not got that pay rise you asked for two years ago. You resent your role, yet you stay and waste all your positive energy on it. You moan to your friends about the situation every time you see them (which annoys them endlessly), and you blame your current company for taking up all your time and preventing you from getting a new job. You've let it consume you, while your confidence has plummeted so low you no longer recognise your own abilities.

So where does that leave you? Clinging onto the job you actually hate doing. A job you know you can do better than – and want to – but your severe lack of confidence makes you feel so low that you can't even detect when you've done a good job, let alone think of applying for a new role.

If you are currently in this state of mind, there's no two ways about it: you're in a crap place. But the one thing I tell myself (and others who find themselves in the clinger camp) is that you are in control of your emotions – and, most importantly, your actions. You have to stop playing the blame game. You can keep working late, holding out for that pay rise, and wait longingly for your hard work to be recognised. Or you can take a real hard look at the situation and admit it's not making you happy. You have to climb out of that godawful hole and recognise that in this case the grass really is greener, and you deserve better. Recognising that this state of unhappiness isn't necessary, acceptable or how you want to live your life is crucial.

So what can you do about it? A small but effective thing is keeping a record of the highs and lows of work. Whether it's in a little black book or just in your iPhone Notes app, it can help to write things down as they happen. It was this technique that helped me escape a dead-end job with a bully of a boss at the start of my career. The reasons for the endless months of crying all became clear when I reread my logged work dramas; and writing them down helped me acknowledge that my emotions weren't just the result of 'that time of the month' – it really was my unbearable boss ruining my life. When the facts, good and bad, are in front of you, it makes it easier to detect patterns and identify what the real problems are.

2. WHERE THE FUCK DO I START?

Once you've identified something needs to change because you're sick of ranting to everyone you see, including the guy you buy your lunch off in Pret, the next stage is admitting that you have no idea where to start. You've spent so long out of the game, you don't know how to be 'in the game'. You don't know what you need to do to get noticed and you don't want to ask your friends or colleagues in case you look incapable; you're seeing your peers start their own businesses, but you feel like you can't even match your shoes to your outfit without feeling overwhelmed. You desperately want to start changing your situation, but you don't know how to use your time to make that happen. You're surrounded by these apparent superstars who somehow go to the gym, work two jobs, have a social life, look presentable, eat well – and look like they're loving it. Seriously, who are these people?

You start working on one goal and then jump to the next when you get stuck, so you never actually finish what you need to do to get started. You have bought every self-help book out there, you've attended empowering career events and your podcast playlist couldn't be more inspirational if it was curated by Oprah herself, but you've still not put your words into action and made a change.

I want to tell you now, this is a very common conundrum. Particularly when no one is there to coach you through it. You feel lonely, lost and frustrated that you can't seem to get out of the mess you've found yourself in. But the great news is, you're out of clinger camp and on the right path. Mind-map everything you want to do, and prioritise what you can realistically focus on at this moment in time. This could be influenced by your current schedule, your access to certain tools, or simply the positive impact completing a particular task might have on your well-being. Remember, you don't have to have all the solutions. No one does. You've just got to break away from your commitment issues and jump head first into taking control of your goals.

3. PROCRASTINATING PERFECTIONISM

If you're naturally a perfectionist, you'll spend a hell of a lot of time protesting that your work is 'not quite finished yet'. The problem is it will *never* be 'good enough' for you to share. You put an intense amount of pressure on yourself to only show the very best of your work, and thus pre-emptively reject yourself before others get the chance. You assume you know what a potential client or employer is looking for, and try to cover all bases without even knowing if what you're doing is right or wrong. You won't give yourself a deadline because you know you won't meet it, so you're in this never-ending cycle of not putting yourself out there – just in case it doesn't truly represent your skills or people don't like your work. Before you know it, six months have gone by and you've done zilch about getting yourself out there. You've got nothing to show for staying in all those Saturday nights, but when people ask you how it's going, you reply with, 'Great, I'm nearly done,' knowing full well that's an absolute lie.

This can't go on any longer. Your fear of only putting your best version of yourself out there on display will mean you continue to miss opportunities, like applying for jobs, chasing after new work or speaking up about your passions, and forever remain invisible. You have to learn to move past this form of perfectionism, and make sure people know what your talents are – before it's too late and you wind up being that person who had all the potential but never really made it. Something I encourage a lot of my friends to do is to go ahead and create a portfolio or platform, but keep it a secret and don't feel the pressure to publicise until you're comfortable with it. The important thing is that you have put pen to paper (or however you choose to create) – it will prevent your ideas getting so lost inside that head of yours that they become a distant memory of something you could have had.

COMPETENCE VS CONFIDENCE

All three of the confidence barriers I've just outlined are influenced by the competence/confidence cycle. I first read about this in Caroline Foran's *The Confidence Kit* (a must-read for anyone who wants to overcome a lack of confidence), in which she explains that most of us increase in confidence only as we increase our competence. However, the people who accelerate fastest through their careers are the ones who have self-confidence irrespective of whether they have proven they are competent enough to completely nail the task at hand. A belief that it's okay to attempt something without knowing the outcome – and a willingness to take that risk – is more important than a perfect skillset. So often I see people not applying for jobs, not winning new business and not living life to the fullest, all because they worry too much about being perfectly skilled before they even begin.

Take my friend Sarah, for example: an aspiring entertainment queen, she was on cloud nine about DJing an East London R&B and hip-hop night until she was told she had been given the headline slot. She came to me in a complete frenzy, having already convinced herself that she couldn't take it on. Now, I might not be completely down with the music scene, but I'm pretty sure there was no difference in the music she was going to play at 10.30 p.m. versus what she was going to play at 12.30 a.m., so what was she so frantic about? Well, she said, it was the feeling that she hadn't earned her place in a high-profile spot. What would people say about her if she messed up or just wasn't up to scratch? This was her first official gig; she thought she couldn't be thrown that far into the deep end on day one.

I explained to her two things: 1. She would always be an opening act if she didn't put herself forward and own the floor at midnight; and 2. Everyone's drunker by then, so she just needed to make sure she played some legendary bangers and she'd be a star. I'm proud to report (and remember) that she did, and she was. Since unlocking that self-belief and continuing to practise her craft, over the past 12 months she has played for global brands and bagged a slot at the Ministry of Sound on NYE. She'll be the first to say she's still learning, but the difference is, she is putting herself out there simultaneously.

You could spend your entire life waiting to perfect a skill – and in doing so, miss out on the chance to discover how good you really are. I'm sure you've heard them all before, but there's truth to the sayings 'Be it until you see it', 'Fake it until you make it' and, my personal mantra, 'Blag now, worry later'. I can guarantee that if you give blagging a go now, you'll be surprised that you don't need to ever worry later, because you *do* have the skills in place. When you read about the biggest icons in business, they weren't the ones who waited their entire lives to perfect every skill and have every answer; they were the ones who blagged first and figured it out along the way.

People go to great lengths to get the dream jobs they want, and if you're desperate to change your current situation it's important you think alternatively to cut through. One of my favourite interviews with Lady Gaga is when she admitted to putting on an English accent pretending to be her own manager, and even used the words, 'She's really hot right now' when pitching herself for gigs. Imagine how hilariously mortifying that would be if you ever got caught out? But the reality is she didn't. There are so many stories out there of successful people who put everything into their self-belief and it's the reason we admire them today.

Now, I'm not encouraging you to talk about yourself in the third person as 'hot right now', but what I'm highlighting is that sometimes you've just got to wing it to win it. There's a whole world out there for you to experience, but it will remain untouched and undiscovered if you never allow yourself the chance to embrace it. You should not be constrained by your mindset, your current environment or the past. When it comes down to it, you are the only thing holding yourself back in your situation – and only you can make the changes to improve it.

Rob More sums it up perfectly in his book *Start Now. Get Perfect Later*: 'You probably weren't perfect the first time you had sex, but that didn't stop you from having a go.' So, now I've got you having flashbacks of your cringy sexual encounters, I'd say it's time to move on to the next chapter.

I asked rising stars a series of questions and have included their best answers throughout the book to inspire readers.

NAFISA BAKKAR

CEO of Amaliah.com

What's one of your best attributes and how did you figure it out?

'What I find really interesting is that there's a stat out there that says when you ask people what they're terrified of, public speaking comes above death – and that's how terrified people are of public speaking. I think a part of it is because people don't really get an opportunity to public-speak, so I'm really grateful I had the opportunity while I was studying at university. I was part of a society called Enactus at UCL, and we had to do public speaking in front of panels, judges and audiences. I'm an introvert, and I used to think I'd have to be a theatrical speaker in order to look confident and be able to engage an audience, but I have really become comfortable with my style – which is understated. I'm confident and I don't need to speak louder, or shout; I'm just confident with what I'm saying and that comes across now.'

How can people embrace the saying 'Blag now, worry later?'

'Recently I've been reading the Stormzy book *Rise Up*, and one of the things it says is to get the basics right, turn up on time, do your research, send a follow-up email – those basic things that you're not actually taught but you pick up along the way – and there's so much truth in that. For me, every single meeting I go to, no matter whose court the ball is in, I will always research them, I will always have a way to say "How I can help you?", I will always know what they've done, I will always be on my A game. It's about prepared blagging. It's knowing that if that person asks me a question, I have something to pull out.'

Do you battle with imposter syndrome? If so, what advice would you give to people trying to overcome it?

'I absolutely battle with it! One thing I do when I want to do something but I'm not sure of myself, I have to make it as real as possible. So say I want to do a huge collaboration – I'll basically create artwork and posters for that moment to make it feel real, like "this is happening". It's very powerful if there is something you want to achieve but you haven't embarked on it yet. For me it could be writing a speech, because I'm comfortable with public speaking; for someone else it might be writing a press release or mocking up a visual of that piece of work in a magazine. It's about making the idea a reality so you have the confidence it can happen – because, ultimately, imposter syndrome is steeped in not having enough confidence.'

TWO

KNOWING WHAT YOU STAND FOR

stress to everyone who attends my events: before you even begin thinking about self-promotion, you must first figure out what your dreams are. And no, this is not some wishy-washy self-help exercise for you to dismiss. It's a genuine question – one you've probably not been asked since you were six years old. (I'm going to take a wild guess that you're now out of your 'Premier League footballer' or 'ballerina' phase.)

Other than a slight blip during my teens when I told people I wanted to be a WAG, I quite quickly identified that I knew I wanted to work in the creative industries. When everyone else was preparing for their so-called gap year, I was relentlessly applying for graduate jobs in advertising (none of which I got, by the way). Forever labelled 'the career-driven one' in my friendship group, my ambition of a future in the creative industries was never a secret. But I didn't always think beyond that – to what I really cared about in life, and how work could help me to achieve those things or stand in my way.

It was another book that changed my way of thinking. *The Dream Manager* by Matthew Kelly tells the story of a (fictional) company that is failing to retain its staff. Week on week they are dropping like flies, and it is costing the company time, money and resources. So eventually the managers start asking their departing staff: What is making you want to leave?

Their responses are simple and there is a common theme: they don't feel their dreams will come true there. As in many businesses, the managers initially assume that when people refer to their 'dreams' they are talking about higher salaries, fancy company cars and accelerating to the top. But those aren't what would lead to happiness. For the employees, what matters most are things like taking driving lessons or giving their kids the best possible Christmas.

The business realises that if they can help their staff to achieve these personal dreams, they might have half a chance of keeping them. So they hire a Dream

Manager (a kind of financial planner), who sits down with each employee to map out how they can achieve what is really important to them. Without spoiling the book, through the help of the Dream Manager, first houses are bought, driving tests are passed, and in one story, the whole office clubs together to buy gifts for Bob so he can give his kids the best possible Christmas (this is the point at which I blubbed, mid-flight, as it restored my faith in humanity).

But *The Dream Manager* is not just a lesson on how business owners should invest in staff. The biggest takeaway from the book for me (and for you) is the need to speak your dreams. Where do you want to go? What do you want to do? What do you want to achieve in life? Figuring this out will help you make key decisions about career moves and will be the foundations of your success.

To give you some inspiration, because most people are usually overwhelmed (and even silenced) by the very thought of figuring out their dreams, I'll share three of mine:

1   TO CREATE ADVERTISING THAT CHANGES THE WORLD

I've always known I wanted to work in advertising, but it wasn't until I started a blog while at university that I realised I wasn't into creating ads promoting Ikea's latest flatpack furniture or personalised Coca-Cola bottles.

I launched If It Was My Way (the worst WordPress site you've ever seen – now thankfully lost to the depths of the internet) – having never written a blog before. On it, I just shared things I liked – which was, more often than not, advertising. I started to see a pattern in what I shared, and it was clear that non-profit and behavioural-change advertising was the most compelling to me. From Amnesty International to Patagonia to WaterAid, it was advertising that could make a difference in the world that stole my heart.

So, ever since university, I've been chasing that dream, moving from agency to agency to find a company that shares the same values and has the capabilities and the connections to create world-changing advertising.

It's easy to know you want to work in a particular industry, but it's also easy to find yourself chained down to places that don't reflect what you want to achieve personally. If they're not going to make your dreams come true, then why give your blood, sweat and tears to them five days a week? We all have a reason for doing what we do; you just have to find yours.

2 TO INSPIRE OTHERS THROUGH PUBLIC SPEAKING

I have always been a lover of storytelling, forever opening up social situations with tales of 'Stefisms' (moments that reveal my scattier qualities) or enthusing about things that I'm passionate about – which usually ends up being, you guessed it, my work and side projects.

When I discovered TED Talks, I became completely obsessed: the endless hours of inspiration; the chance to discover topics I never knew I cared about; and the global sharing of ideas. Pretty soon, becoming a TED Speaker became one of my main life goals. The idea that my words could improve another person's life fills me with an overwhelmingly warm feeling, and I've been seeking out opportunities to speak publicly ever since.

So much so that, when I could see that I wasn't being invited to speak at events because of my gender, age and level of experience but knew that I could help others, I set up F*ck

Being Humble and made my own stage. I didn't let others judge whether I was experienced enough by an 'industry standard'; I identified what I was qualified to speak on, created a place to shine and as a result, for the first time ever, started being paid to speak by global brands. Money for talking? In my eyes, that is a dream job come true (and with every hope it will be the springboard to TED one day).

Do what you love and the money will follow. There will be a way to monetise your passions, and things that have only ever been considered personality quirks could be the gateway to your biggest successes.

3 <u>TO TRAVEL</u>

I've been privileged enough to experience some of the most amazing parts of the world – both on holidays and when living abroad during my childhood – so part of what I consider the benchmark of my own success is how many holidays I can go on a year. Not in a competitive, materialistic way, but in a 'I love to experience the world around me' way. That's why, at the time of writing, as many of my friends are putting away money in their first-flat fund, I'm putting money into my early retirement fund to travel the world. For a lot of people, staying in one place and becoming a homeowner is the definition of success; but for me, living in different parts of the world and rewarding my hard work with remote island getaways is the ultimate #lifegoals. Discover your own path, and don't be afraid to follow it. What looks like success to you may be your friend's worst nightmare, but that's okay!

I've only outlined three dreams here (trust me, I have more) because, right now, they are my priority – but I'm also very aware that in time my dreams will change. Something I learned (and accepted) only recently is that expecting your job to be the answer to all your dreams is unrealistic. If you cling to this idea, you're likely to spend the rest of your life pointlessly searching for a 'dream job' that just doesn't exist. It's also okay to have different ambitions at different stages of your life. In fact, it's even more important to recognise that you don't have to do everything you set out to achieve. You don't have to be a prisoner to dreams you identified when you were 16. If they're not serving you anymore and you find that the reality doesn't (or wouldn't) make you happy, then let them go. Be realistic, and review your ambitions regularly.

By mapping out your dreams, you can figure out how and where you can action them. Take my dreams, for example. I was very aware that until I was awarded a managing director role, the likelihood I would get to 'inspire others through public speaking' on behalf of any of the companies I worked for was quite rightly very slim, because I was pretty young and there were more experienced people to represent the business. I could have sat and stewed in resentment that my day job wasn't allowing me to achieve my dreams in life (and trust me, I have done on many occasions), but instead I decided to find a way to make it happen myself.

Another example is a friend of mine, Phoebe. She spent the first five years of her career as an accountant for the ad agency we both worked at, but deep down she always knew she had more of a creative side and that it was being sucked out of her. Photography was something she'd always had an interest in but hadn't considered seriously as a career. She had a style, an edge, and could take a cut-through photo people would actually want to share. She would shoot grime gigs after work and capture intimate festival moments over the weekends, but most importantly she shared them with the outside world via a perfectly visualised Instagram and her own website. She transitioned her reputation from the edgy finance girl to the edgy *photographer* finance girl in no time. And before she knew it, the time she'd invested started to lead to a financial payoff. People were booking her for shoots and she was getting referrals from the jobs she worked on. It made her realise she didn't want to be chained to a desk with Excel as her best mate; she wanted to be a photographer. So she took the leap and went freelance – and while the change wasn't without difficulties, she found something she loved doing.

But before you get too excited by this romantic career-changing whirlwind, Phoebe is also a realist. She knew she still had bills to pay and a life she wanted to lead that, financially, her photographer's salary just wouldn't support. So she filled her days with both freelance accounting and photography shoots. Does she keep on accounting because she still wants to work in finance? No – she does it because she wants to be self-reliant and values having a flat, a car and an ability to travel. But now she has more control over her time and the freedom to pursue her dreams – something that, despite the stability and higher salary, her old job would never have allowed. By prioritising her creative fulfilment and yet being real with herself about her financial needs, Phoebe has found a lifestyle that she could excel in.

Like Phoebe, you might not be living your dreams straight out of the gate, and that is totally fine. Not being on track doesn't mean it can't be done. But you need to sit down and really think: *What do I want my legacy to be? What do I want people to know me for? What do I want to succeed at in life? What will be the driver of my happiness?*

Write down those dreams, and spend a good amount of time thinking about them – because, when you do, you'll feel a whole lot clearer about the next steps.

CRAFTING YOUR STORY

They say university is a place for finding yourself, and I can agree with that whole-heartedly. For example, I found myself putting on two stone from abusing my right to have a Maccies cheeseburger on the side of my 24 Chicken McNuggets meal three times a week. I found I had an unrivalled ability to style charity-shop steals with vintage knock-offs (on reflection, a 'talent' I wish had stayed under wraps). I found that the library, a place I loathed growing up, was actually my saviour. But most importantly, I found that I didn't *really* know how to talk about myself. Not in a way that truly captured my personality, or that would help me to stand out from the hundred other girls around me.

My course, Fashion Communication and Promotion at Nottingham Trent, wasn't a conventional academic degree, and despite what the name would suggest, it more closely resembled three straight years of *The Apprentice* than anything else. We studied theory, of course, but we also learned real-world skills – the stuff you need to survive throughout your career that is so often overlooked – the most valuable being: how to stand up in front of our peers and pitch our ideas, knowing that they would, without fail, be ripped to shreds. We developed thick skins and a relentless ability to bounce back.

As I started on my journey, I thought I was pretty good at selling my ideas (and absolutely anything else) – until, that is, I began the semester on self-promotion in our second year. We were briefed to make logos, business cards, visual CVs and online portfolios nearly two whole years before we would face job-hunting for real. But while we may have been brand-obsessed, the idea of conveying our own *personal* brands through a CV was unanimously daunting.

I'll be honest, I was secretly confident that my CV was pretty good. So far it had got me a job earning minimum wage as a sales assistant at Office and then French Connection, so it had to be good, right? I learned just how wrong I was when a guest lecturer insisted each and every one of us stood up and read out the opening personal profile from our CV. The sheer horror. It's bad enough having to live up to the bigged-up CV version of yourself in an interview – let alone reading out how highly you rate yourself in front of all the intimidatingly cool girls on your course at 19.

One by one, with our hands shaking and our anxiety levels through the roof, we mumbled through our profiles, and every time, without fail, our lecturer's response was: 'That was shit, sit down and start writing a new one.' It was how I envisaged hell would be, and it didn't stop there. We were collectively made to rewrite – and reshare – our bios at least three times, until we finally got to a point where our CVs had more character than Kanye circa 2018. The only benefit of the humiliation was that we soon realised the only thing original about us that day were the different-coloured Creepers we were wearing. The people I'd spent 18 months being so intimidated by didn't know how to stand out, and neither did I.

So what was so bad about the CV I rode in on my high horse with that day? Let me show you ...

> *A mature, responsible undergraduate with excellent communication skills, studying a degree in Fashion Communication and Promotion. Confident dealing with people of all ages. Hard worker who values success in all parts of my studies, social and business life.*

That was it.

This did not describe who I was; it missed out all the things that did make me stand out; and it certainly wasn't going to grab the attention of my dream employer. The best advice our lecturer gave us that day was: 'You have to put your personality to paper.' It sounds so simple, so obvious, so easy. But we know that, if it really were that easy, everyone would be living their best lives in their first jobs, knowing they were exactly where they were supposed to be.

I now know how lucky I was to be coached on this, but so many people don't get the chance. Instead, they produce and reproduce soulless descriptions of themselves. I'm forever receiving and reading portfolios, CVs and LinkedIn profiles that lack any form of life, and it's even harder when I know the person and know how much potential is hidden inside that terrible cover note.

It's important to remember that people make assumptions and judgements during their first interaction with you, whether that be digitally or physically. And the earliest assessments people make of you are often the ones they stick to, so if they decide you're boring at the beginning, they'll subconsciously find evidence to back that characterisation up – or, worse still, dismiss you altogether.

This is what we call 'confirmation bias'. In the *Guardian* article 'Acting on Impulse', Rosie Ifould explores the research and impact of our snap decision-making when it comes to strangers. She gave the example that after meeting a friend's new boyfriend, you might decide he's a little aloof. From then on, you will be on the lookout for other signs of that aloofness, noticing when he blanks someone else at a party or doesn't offer to buy a round at the pub. But you won't necessarily notice if he offered to buy a round and everyone declined. We seek out the information that tells us we are right, and we ignore or assign little importance to anything that might suggest otherwise. So it's important to cut through the shit right off the bat, and serve your genuine self on a plate.

With this in mind, remember that anything you show to someone you're trying to impress could be the thing that defines you in their eyes for some time. Now, because I don't want to send you back to the 'Where the fuck do I start?' zone, I want to explain the common pitfalls I see when I receive a piece of writing that I know isn't doing that person justice.

YOU'RE BEING TOO LITERAL

I can't tell you how many CVs I read that feel like they've been written by an Alexa. You spell out the obvious, name-drop if you can, and that's it. I know within 10 seconds that you're looking for a job in music production because that is the title of your email, so why have you repeated it again and wasted valuable page space? You haven't made me smile, and I won't remember you 10 minutes later. I know it sounds blunt, but tell me why you love music in a way I've not read before. Make me sit up and listen!

If you've never read Simon Sinek's *Start With Why*, I highly recommend you do so now. The overall premise is that everyone and everything has a purpose in life. Think about why you work in your industry – what makes you get out of bed in the morning to do your job. Is there a problem you want to change? Have you always been obsessed with the industry? Is it a new obsession? What is it that makes you tick? If, like many people, you need a little inspiration to guide you on your way, take a look at these heart-warming examples from some of my good friends to remind you that everyday people can find their purpose too ...

• IT'S IN MY BLOOD

Hannah was in meltdown when the hair salon she worked at closed. She was forced to set up as a freelancer, and needed to find her point of difference in an overly cluttered beauty industry. So I asked her a simple question: when was the first time you realised you really wanted to be a hairdresser? Her response was perfect. She described an early memory of being told to dress up as her dream job in primary school; aged eight, she rolled into class sporting a belt filled with combs, brushes and scissors, a hairdryer in hand (picture a *Ghostbusters* pose).

But this story wasn't just a cute Throwback Thursday moment; it was proof that her passion for styling hair was firmly rooted in her life – something she'd formed an interest in at a young age and pursued 10 years later. That anecdote showed decisiveness, commitment and an undeniable affinity with the industry she was in.

AN INSPIRATION

Not all stories are like Hannah's. You might have changed your mind a hundred times and still have no idea what your dream job is – let alone be working in it. But there are things, people and issues that could yet inspire you to embrace an opportunity you may never have considered. After attending a workshop I hosted, Sylvia reached out to me to review a cover note and CV she'd written to apply for a job at *Vogue*. What was different about Sylvia's story was that she'd spent the past five years training as a paralegal and was making the ambitious leap into a new career as a self-taught photographer. Aside from her well-developed portfolio, I was most impressed with how she conveyed her need to work at *Vogue* now more than ever: it was the work of Edward Enninful, the magazine's recently appointed first black editor-in-chief, who was challenging a white-washed industry to be more racially inclusive – and, in particular, a recent speech he'd given in Accra, at the Jubilee House – that Sylvia connected with the most. As a Nigerian creative, she finally had a role model in her field effecting change that she personally connected with, and it was this that gave her the courage to reach out to one of the biggest media powerhouses in the world – regardless of her creative industry qualifications. It is through these stories that employers can learn more about what your drive and motivations are in life. People thrive off connection, so always try to find what connects you and make it clear to them.

How can you lead with emotion like Sylvia? Who has had an inspirational impact on your life, good or bad? Is there something that drove you to pursue a certain path – and, if so, how can you integrate that into your personal story?

The more you show off your character, the more people will have an opportunity to empathise with you. They might find similarities or be moved by your story, but this can only happen if you take the time to figure out why you love what you do.

YOU MUST HAVE AMNESIA

You've forgotten to write down the things you do daily. The things that are actually really impressive and would wow anyone the first time they read your CV. You've not mentioned anything about your achievements in life, the hard times you've been through, or the hobbies you work your arse off at outside your day job. You've forgotten to explain your character and it's the most important part of the process, so I thought I'd share a few things to consider when it comes to including your *actual* personality:

- ### WHAT DO YOU DO THAT EVERYONE ELSE DOESN'T?

  Whether it's living abroad or writing blogs or teaching dance classes, you might not see why your past experiences or the activities you do in your spare time would be related to potential job opportunities – but they are, trust me. Sharing this information could be a deciding factor in being selected for a role or closing a deal. Also think about the non-work-related tasks you do, and analyse the skills needed to carry them out. Living abroad shows me you're likely to be able to adapt well to new environments; writing blogs demonstrates an ability to curate or to express an opinion; and teaching dance classes shows leadership skills and a teamwork mentality. This is your chance to offer an insight into your character and demonstrate how your personal skills might contribute to the opportunity you're applying for – even indirectly.

• <u>AN OPPORTUNITY TO BRAG</u>

The cynic in you will hate the thought of bragging about your achievements, but if you want to be the one candidate the interviewer is still thinking about when they eat their dinner at night, it's time to get your head out of your 'my work will speak for itself' arse. If you've won an award for your incredible animation skills, write it down. If you've passed exams that you didn't need to sit, write it down. If you worked on something that is uncommon in the industry, write it down. (I'm sure you're getting the gist of this ...)

<u>YOU'RE USING BASIC LANGUAGE</u>

When it comes to descriptive words, it turns out we choose the least disruptive ones to talk about ourselves. I know this from reading lots of personal bios, but this is especially apparent during my workshops, when I ask everyone to stay standing if they use any of the following words to describe themselves:

* Passionate   * Confident   * Strategic   * Creative
* Hard-working * Friendly   * Enthusiastic * Motivated

Every time, 100 per cent of the attendees stay standing. It's only a short experiment, because everyone hates crowd participation, but it's an important one in order for people to wake up and realise: *How can you stand out when you're using the exact same words as everyone else?*

And now I'll set you a very simple task … Get a pen and paper and write a no-filter list of all the words you would use to describe your personality. The good, the bad and everything in between. Don't overthink it, and keep going until you have at least 10 words on the page. The only catch? They can't be any of the words listed above. If you need support flexing your mind, look at a thesaurus or right-click for synonyms if you need to. And if you're getting stuck for whatever reason, don't be afraid to ask your friends, co-workers, family or a partner (from experience, they don't hold back!). Without getting too Pinterest mood-boardy on you, you can even look at icons or brands that you admire and the language they use, and if it applies to you, then steal it. Nobody owns words; you just need to make sure they reflect who you really are. (No employer wants to be catfished.)

Paul Ingram, the Kravis Professor of Business at Columbia Business School, has spent more than 10 years teaching a programme that helps senior global leaders explore their values. His technique is to get them to write down eight key values on a 'Values Card', explaining that, 'Your values are your internal control system … [and what] we rely on to guide us.' By clearly noting down and understanding our values, we're able to make better decisions about our future.

The process is so valuable to his students that he often finds they are still carrying their Values Card with them years later, despite knowing them off by heart. So while it might seem an odd process, identifying words that resonate with you – and keeping them close – can be a powerful way to get comfortable with what makes you stand out.

Once you've got your list of words, think about how you can add them to your vocab when you speak about yourself. Instead of writing 'I'm a designer that loves working on skate culture', you could write something like: 'I'm a designer with an unhealthy obsession and fascination with documenting the world of skate culture'. All of a sudden, I feel way more compelled to learn more about you. And if you must use words like 'passionate' and 'enthusiasm', try to find other descriptive words to add to make them feel less generic.

'YOU TALKING TO ME?'

If you have a creative mind, reading an economic report might feel like a never-ending punishment. Likewise, if you're an academic, reading *Bridget Jones's Diary* might infuriate you beyond belief. That's why the tone and words you use should feel appropriate to the industry and people you are targeting. Don't throw every piece of jargon you've ever heard of onto your CV, but do think about the person who will be reading it. If it's a director at Unilever, you might use different language than if you were writing a bio for an event hosted by Buzzfeed. It's about knowing your audience and speaking their language.

I once read a CV that claimed the applicant was 'eloquent'. Once I met the candidate in person, I completely understood why they'd written it, but it's not necessarily the word I would have used for that role in that industry. Eloquence is not something I'd go searching for and nor would I see it as a deciding factor in employing someone, so it's worth considering the words you use and what they mean to people. That example could have been much more compelling if they'd expressed why their eloquence would be of value in the role and field they were applying for.

FIND A FILTER

When you've got your CV or bio to a place that you're happy with, share it with your nearest and dearest. Stop with that cringe face that I know you're pulling, and pass it to someone who knows you. They don't need to rewrite it or even understand your industry, but if they can confirm that it captures your personality and your individual quirks, you've done a good job.

SELL YOUR BENEFITS, NOT JUST YOUR FEATURES

When you really look into Apple and Samsung's constant battle to dominate the mobile phone market, you'll find that Samsung's products have actually overtaken the quality and performance of Apple's – however, many of us choose not to believe it. For all the frustrating problems that an iPhone presents – low battery, limited storage, screens that smash easily – Samsung has solutions. But the one thing Samsung hasn't managed to perfect is winning hearts over minds. While Samsung might run campaigns that take over Times Square with billboards displaying beautifully slick imagery, accompanied with the line 'Do bigger things', Apple is busy sharing the amazing photography captured by their own customers, showing how the product enabled them to *actually* 'do bigger things'. Samsung tells; Apple shows.

What can you learn from this example? Well, I'm forever meeting with people who just state what they do, not why they make things so great. Again, it comes down to a humble-pie approach and the fact that most of us aren't very good at recognising or even remembering our own contributions to a project. Women in particular are better at identifying talent in others than they are in themselves. Social psychologist Adam Galinsky calls it 'the mama bear effect' – women champion others so they don't come across as self-interested, whereas men tend to overestimate their performance by about 30 per cent (according to a

Columbia Business School study). Good for you, men; it's obviously working for you. Women, take note.

All too often, we focus only on commentating and not enough on storytelling. We'll talk about the story factually, but not the reason it ended up increasing revenue by 50 per cent. And we won't mention that if it wasn't for our involvement, there would be no repeat business, the project wouldn't look as good as it does and the company wouldn't be proudly sharing our work as a case study.

You might be petrified of coming across like you think you're God's gift, but that's not what this exercise of crafting your achievements is about; it's about looking at your contribution, its positive results and understanding how best to communicate what you bring to the table.

When I was 16, I worked for Barratts Shoes (a British high-street footwear retailer that was not exactly the most glam) and we were forced to sell shoe care. You know, the suede protective spray that you never want to buy? Well, if you were the lowest 'shoe-care seller of the day', you'd have to vacuum the shop floor. In hindsight, I'm not sure they were legally allowed to do that, but I did it anyway for about eight weeks straight. Until, one day, I got sick of dragging Henry the Hoover around the obstacle course of a shop floor, and I decided to learn every single detail about the shoe-care products. You name it, I knew it. It was no longer an add-on to the transaction; it was embedded in sealing the entire deal. I researched what would happen to the shoes if people didn't buy the product, and would select a specific problem to pull out, depending on the customer. I eventually became the top shoe-care seller, my Henry days long behind me. While it might not have been an obvious career-changing moment, I still tell that story in interviews today because it's an insight into my commitment to a business and a goal. It's not about me becoming the top seller; it's the journey I went through to get there.

So let's look at how you might take a professional example currently on your CV and improve it by moving from commentating to storytelling. Your current description might read something like one I used to include:

> I project-managed the production of the university prospectus, including photography, design and copy.

There is no denying that this is true information, but it's very literal. It doesn't explain why my involvement in particular had an impact on the project I work on or the business I worked for.

With your own examples you need to give a sense of what was involved during the project management process. Was it a short deadline? How much did you produce? How has it affected the client or company you were working for? What did you do to go above and beyond? With this filter, let's try that again:

> To deliver a real overview of the university's offering, I conducted 17 interviews over four weeks which influenced the entire creative and content direction of the prospectus and other brand communications. Alongside this, I coordinated three shoots, managed external suppliers and delivered the client an asset bank of over 300 pieces of content.

Can you see the difference? By reviewing the process that you went through to create the work you're so proud of, you can immediately elevate your involvement by highlighting areas that you know the person reading will be impressed by. I'm not saying that when people ask you about a recent project you should reel off every single minute detail, but having it thought through in your mind is a great way to ensure you're prepared for any opportunities you have to share. It's kind of like when you see an ex-flame, they ask what you've been up to and your reply is 'not much' – which of course doesn't impress, and nor is it going to make them want to jump back into your arms. Then, 10 minutes later, you think of a million other things you've done and could have bragged about that would have sounded so much better than 'not much'.

It's worth keeping a list of the exciting things you've done recently, so you're always equipped. By turning an experience into a story, it makes it more enjoyable for whoever's reading it, and you start to recognise and convey your value more clearly – which is not only important for when you've got to fill an awkward silence in an interview or pitch, but is also essential for getting the recognition and money you deserve (we'll get into this in more detail in Chapter 6).

The way you choose to keep track of your input is totally up to you. But by documenting your achievements only when you're applying for a new job or pitching to a prospective client, you can run the risk of overlooking key contributions that demonstrate your ability. To be on the safe side, I'd recommend doing monthly reviews of what's going well, and what you could be learning from or improving. The more you reflect, the fresher your achievements will be in your mind – and you won't miss the opportunity to share when the time comes.

Now, don't freak out because you're not already doing this stuff. It's like I said at the start of the book, if no one has ever taught you how to talk about yourself, how can you be expected to already be good at it? In an ideal world, you would have someone constantly telling you all the amazing things you bring to the table, but the reality is this type of analysis depends on you giving yourself the time and recognising what makes your craft truly unique.

LEYYA SATTAR AND ROSHNI GOYATE

Founders of The Other Box

——

What's your top trick to be remembered for what you do; how do you position yourself in a unique way?

'This is going to sound so cheesy, but you should just be yourself. This is how people are going to remember you. When I first graduated, my design portfolio was terrible and mainly filled with creative projects I'd worked on at university and "freelance" work I had done on one of those websites where they pay you £3 for a logo! My first boss in the industry didn't hire me because of this terrible portfolio but said (years later) it was because she could see the passion, ambition and fire I had. We would also say keep it simple – have a direct, strong message, and support it with stories that spark inspiration in others and show your humanity. Just like the one we've just told, in fact!'

When was a time where you blagged your way through something and it paid off? How can people embrace the saying 'Blag now, worry later?'

'When we first started The Other Box, we weren't sure what it was going to be exactly, only that we needed to start *something* to address the lack of diversity in the creative industries. To help gain traction, we took every opportunity to be on diversity panels, get interviewed for various diversity features, and basically spread our message, to let people know we were starting something and we had big aspirations. When we look back on some of those, we can see how green we were and how much our brand and business have developed since then, but if we hadn't taken the plunge with those speaking opportunities in the first place, we wouldn't be where we are today!'

Getting the money you deserve can be tricky. What's the best money advice you could give to get what you're worth?

'Talk about money! Whether you're freelancing or in a permanent position, talk to your friends and peers about money and research your position online to see what the going rate is. The research will give you the data to back up whatever fee or salary you're negotiating, but also give you the confidence in getting paid what you deserve. We also suggest being more mindful of your spending habits, so take a little time each month to track and review your money, to see what your general expenses are. You can then evaluate where you can cut back if you need to, and what you can put away as savings.'

THREE

DON'T BE
IN HIDING

---

nce you get comfortable with identifying key words that describe you, and talking about your various achievements and what it is that makes them so special, it's time to make sure people *actually* see them. And I'm not just talking about updating your CV; I'm talking about being searchable in the right places in order to put you in a prime position for any future opportunities.

THE CURRENT CLIMATE

Have you ever done that thing when you meet someone at a party, find out their name, search for their social media handle, and then relentlessly stalk them to decide whether you were a victim of vodka goggles or they really are the person you're going to marry? If you're not nodding along, you're obviously more trusting than most – because for many of us social media detectives, the way a potential romantic candidate positions themselves on social media can be the deciding factor in whether you ever speak to them again. Yes, we're judgemental, and yes, they could be an amazing person with little experience of the online stalking process, but ultimately it is the reality of today's world. With social media platforms and search engines at our fingertips more than ever before, the ability to judge a book by its cover has never been so prevalent. And while I wish I could say I'm shocked at the behaviour and don't do it personally, I'd be lying.

And it isn't just romantic leads – it's professional ones too. In fact, my boyfriend often laughs at the amount of LinkedIn notifications I get (even over the week-end), notifying me that someone has recently viewed my profile. The difference with LinkedIn is you can actually track who's looking!

During the widely accepted – and even expected – stalking process, you are critiqued in all manner of ways: on the people you're in photos with, the people you're connected with, the articles you like, the things you comment on and how closely your digital persona matches the real-life version of you. It is through this online vetting that people form initial opinions of you. It is the digital validation process, and it's going absolutely nowhere.

But as Mark Schaefer, author of *Known: The Handbook for Building and Unleashing Your Personal Brand in the Digital Age*, says, there's a difference between being 'internet famous' and curating a specific personal brand that will help you become known in your industry. You might not want to be an Insta-star, especially as you can see how hard that is to maintain and how easily you can be scrutinised for it, but using social media to carve out a reputation and build a presence in your industry can be transformative for your career. A previous boss of mine openly admitted that, after stalking me on social media and learning more about my personality, she knew I'd be right for the job. (Luckily, I'd just been to New York and purchased a film camera, so my feed was full of grainy street photography – as opposed to my older, mundane, hangover-breakfast posts.)

But it's not just about being 'visually' pleasing; it's about demonstrating your skills to those who otherwise might not get to experience them or see them to their full extent. Having a podcast linked to your online profile can give an actual voice to your paper CV; having a blog where you share your unfiltered opinions can demonstrate your ability to write with passion; and having an online portfolio listing your projects not only makes it easier for a potential employer or client to see everything you've worked on in one place, but is also a way of referencing all the people you've worked with, which can help build your status at the same time. We have to stop looking at online reputation as something only celebrities need to consider; it's for everyone – including you. In an interview with London-based artist Kelly Anna, she explained that when she wants to work with specific brands she doesn't always hound them to get noticed. Her current passions are sports and producing art murals, so she will intentionally post visuals of her work that includes both so that people start recognising her for that. Her consistent sharing of commissioned work, passion projects, bespoke merch and live installations have all led to brands reaching out to her instead of her needing to chase them. It sounds so simple, but you have the ability to shape how people perceive your capabilities to work in line with your preferences; you just have to be tactical about it.

Now, while I'm not going to judge semi-naked photos of your perfectly sculpted bum or question why you're still awake posting videos at 6 a.m., it is worth remembering that if we're all using the power of the web to check the compatibility of future partners, you can bet the same is being done for potential employees. Whether it's a simple Google search, a sneak peak of your LinkedIn profile or reading your endless waffling tweets, pretty much anyone who isn't living under a rock will look you up online before agreeing to connect with you.

But what are they looking for? Well, research from the employment website CareerBuilder lists the top three reasons employers check up on prospects:

1 **TO SEE IF THE JOB SEEKER PRESENTS HIMSELF OR HERSELF PROFESSIONALLY**

2 **TO KNOW IF THE CANDIDATE IS A GOOD FIT FOR THE COMPANY CULTURE**

3 **TO LEARN MORE ABOUT HIS OR HER QUALIFICATIONS**

According to a *Harvard Business Review* article '70% of employers who have used LinkedIn say they've chosen not to hire a person based on what they've found out about them online'. So while you might feel the voyeuristic approach is unnecessary or even intrusive, for employers it saves time and energy, and can prepare them for the otherwise unseen.

That one post could influence whether you're considered a competitive candidate – but then, so could the lack of posts. You can't be 'discovered' if you're nowhere to be found ...

HOW NARCISSISM COULD BE OUR SAVIOUR

They say we're the most narcissistic generation yet, but our narcissism could well be the differentiator between having a strong online profile and being digitally invisible. It could even, in fact, be the thing that gets us the job over someone else.

What I've observed is that our desire to share our 'best lives' usually only extends to champagne-popping Boomerangs and posting photos of our new trainers. But our obsession with our appearance online – from colour-coordinating posts to memorising our number of followers – could actually signify a level of self-awareness we need to keep us on track.

As we explored in Chapter 2, we so often suffer from a paralysis and embarrassment that holds us back from putting our work online for the world to judge. But just as our offline life involves both work and play, so should our social media platforms. For many of us, our work is culturally relevant, important to society and would be another opportunity for our peers to connect with. We are more than just bottomless brunches and dog walks; we put so much of our time and energy into our jobs, passions and side projects. We've earned the right to share these things – and we *should* share them.

In this section, we're going to explore how to prep your online persona so you can hit the ground running with a consistent, honest representation of you that you can own.

WHAT DOES EVERYONE ELSE SEE?

I'll ask you a question: when was the last time you googled yourself, and what did you find when you did? If a stream of outdated social media profiles with some questionable dusty-mirror selfies popped up, then it's time to pay a bit more attention to your online reputation. When I decided to do this, it wasn't just my vanity that made an unwanted comeback, it was my first-year university project: although I was proud of it at the time, it didn't quite illustrate my skills as an advertising account director six years later. If you're not updating your profiles regularly, it's easy for amateur work to become the only representation of yourself.

Now, before you smugly sit back because a shameful selfie or embarrassing project didn't pop up, don't think that you've got out of this. In fact, if your Google search served up the hundreds of other people with your name – from ex-convicts to doctors – and your profile was nowhere to be seen, then I'd say you've got even more work to be doing.

If you want to be taken seriously in your chosen field, you've got to start treating your profile with care, because if you don't, no one else will. Here are the common pushbacks I hear when it comes to bad online presences, and every time it frustrates me greatly because they are weak excuses with immediate solutions.

10 EXCUSES FOR NOT HAVING A REPRESENTATIVE ONLINE PROFILE (AND WHY THEY'RE NOT GOOD ENOUGH)

1   I don't have time. *(It doesn't have to be a lot of time – just turn off Netflix for one night.)*

2   I don't know what to include. *(The stuff you feel is most representative of your abilities.)*

3   I need more experience. *(... said every procrastinator ever. It's not about quantity, it's about quality.)*

4   I don't want to look arrogant. *(You don't have to as long as you don't include a photo of you sat on a throne.)*

5   No one will look at it anyway. *(Well, they won't if it's not there.)*

6   I don't think my work is good enough. *(Says who? It's not always about the output, it's often the process.)*

7   I'm not very technical. *(YouTube, YouTube, YouTube. Pretty much all services have online training videos to help you; if not, call their customer services – no excuses.)*

8   I don't know what platform to use. *(Whatever you feel most comfortable with staying on top of and which will have the most reach.)*

9   They'll ask if they want to see it. *(They still don't know who you are, so how can they ask?!)*

10   I don't know where to start. *(Well, you're in good hands. Keep and use this book like a bible, working through the chapters.)*

CONSTRUCTING YOUR ONLINE PRESENCE

We can all come up with endless excuses for why our portfolio is still not done or our website is still under construction, but what you have to realise is that a lack of preparation could cost you an opportunity or even your professional credibility. Put it like this – if you met Ryan Gosling and he asked for your number but you didn't have a mobile phone, do you think he'd find other ways to contact you, or move on to the next adoring fan? Do me a favour, avoid a Gos-so-long situation and just be prepared. I promise you that once you have everything set up, you'll feel so much more confident in putting yourself out there – and then it's just a matter of updating every six months or so. Below are the key steps to making sure your online presence brings to life who you really are ...

THE ONLINE CLEAN-UP

First things first – it's important that you review everything currently being served up about you online. Just like an end-of-year clothes cleanse or deep fridge clean, you need to decide what you want to keep and what needs to be chucked out. When I did the dreaded Google search, I realised that the website I'd created including all my projects wasn't showing up on the first page of search results, and having invested a lot of time in making that site, I was pretty annoyed it was on page three after my Bebo page (a nice noughties flashback for all you millennials). What that did encourage me to do was to look at the SEO (search engine optimisation) of the site, and figure out how I could stop some of the unwanted content appearing. It may sound like I had prior knowledge of SEO, but I didn't – at all. I literally watched step-by-step videos and read endless articles online. It's simple things like naming your uploaded images with your own name instead of 'screen-shot-0990430'. Small changes can make a difference!

Stalk yourself regularly; it's not only socially acceptable, it's necessary.

TACTICS FIRST

I'm regularly asked things like, 'If I'm a writer, do I need to have an Instagram account?' With the busy lives that we lead, I can totally understand why you'd be questioning the best place to spread your message. Ultimately, it's about investing your time in the platforms that are most relevant to your industry and that you also enjoy using. It's really important to get this formula right because you might love talking to yourself on Twitter, but if you're a film director, having a profile on Vimeo might be a better use of your time. Similarly, if that platform doesn't come naturally to you, don't kid yourself that you'll keep up with it. Don't worry about being a multi-channel guru on every single platform out there; choose the channels you feel fit your skills, have a connection to your industry and that you know you can frequently update without feeling overwhelmed.

FIGURE OUT YOUR TONE

Chapters 1 and 2 should have given you the tools to position yourself and your personal abilities, so now it's about clearly applying your voice on your chosen platform(s), but please, whatever you do, don't just include your name, role and contact details in your 'About me' section. Put across your personality, make it fun, make it memorable.

Just a word of warning: it's okay to adapt your tone on a channel-by-channel basis, but be careful with leaving platforms unused or incomplete. It makes you look inconsistent, and if it's the only platform I land on, I might automatically dismiss you as you won't come across as very present. Like I said before, no one is asking you to dominate across each and every channel. Just make sure you direct people to a place they can be impressed by.

SOME WORK IS BETTER THAN NO WORK

For all you procrastinating perfectionists out there, you're going to hate this – but having one page with placeholder content is better than having nothing at all. Don't worry, it doesn't have to have a list of 50 industry-changing projects on there; in fact, I always suggest that it's better to share two or three pieces of representative work that you are most proud of than drowning people with outdated weak examples (no one needs to see your first photoshoot with your pet turtle).

Don't let not being an immediate success in your field or not having award-winning work be a barrier to spreading your message across platforms.

FILL IN THE BLANKS

Managing your online profile – whether it's updating your portfolio or pushing out content – isn't easy to stay on top of. Which is why, when you do invest your time into it, make sure what you're putting up there is relevant and clearly demonstrates your involvement. I can't tell you how many websites and portfolios I see that include beautiful imagery but don't actually explain what you did to make the work so great. Of course an end product can look amazing, but it could be even more impressive if you explain the process of getting there (a bit like exams when the teachers used to say it doesn't matter if the final answer isn't right, you still get points for showing your workings out).

A top tip to help take visitors on a journey is to document different aspects of your work. Could you share the different stages of your research? Behind the scenes content? Interviews you conducted? Resources you used, books, podcasts and tech that you used? What lengths did you go to to get the job done?

All this information helps paint a bigger picture of how you approach finding a solution – you never know what might connect with people.

MAKE IT A HABIT

I know it's easier said than done, because as I sit here writing this I can think of projects that I haven't yet updated on my website (I am human!), but the more regularly you devote time to adding content to your channels, the less likely it is that you'll feel overwhelmed by it as it won't be such a beast of a job to do. I personally find that when I'm proud of a project, I want to shout about it. I add it to my platforms almost immediately and try to share it across my social channels. Ride that momentum when you've got it, and set quarterly (or even monthly) reminders to update.

UNDERSTAND YOUR REACH

When I launched FBH, I wrote an article on LinkedIn called 'Why I launched a self-promotion platform called "F*ck Being Humble"'. Granted it wasn't the most original title, but in a constant stream of expected professional development advice, my article cut through. It was read by over 4,000 people globally, liked and commented on internationally – and it even got hateful comments, which is when I really knew I was on to something. There was no paid spend, I didn't tag people in the post, it was all organic reach.

And it was this article that opened the doors to further media coverage and collaborations. That one hour spent writing the original article resulted in several weeks' worth of benefits.

Documenting and recognising the circumstances in which you get the most reach is really beneficial when you're trying to increase engagement. Track what content generates the most interest: what the topic was, when was it posted, what types of people engaged with it, etc. It's not always about who you know; sometimes, just sometimes, it's about what you know too.

LINK IT UP

I recently read an article in which the journalist criticised an out-of-office email they'd received because as well as including their 'I'm on vacay' message, they'd also used the opportunity to direct people to view their latest pieces of work via their personal website. The writer of the article had a slightly archaic attitude and completely disapproved of this type of self-promotion. But my thoughts were that it was bloody genius. It's not intrusive, it's polite and it does a better job of potentially securing a project for you than no message at all. Plus it means you can continue sipping margaritas on the beach while people peruse your work – surely that's a win-win all round?

My thinking is, there is absolutely no point in preparing these platforms if you just hide them away, hoping that someone asks you for them one day. (Remember what I said earlier: your assumption that this will happen is actually more arrogant than just going ahead and sharing your work.) Put your URLs and profile names in your bios and link your social media to your website – this will ensure that, wherever a potential connection lands, they will always be driven back to platforms that are linked to you.

SEND PEOPLE UPDATES

I'm not expecting you to send out a monthly newsletter, but I can't tell you how priceless it is to send out update emails when you've revamped a website or put up new work. The world flashes past us in a second, and as much as you might like to think your dream employer or client has calendar reminders set to constantly check your website for updates, they don't. Do them a favour and slide into their DMs with a gentle reminder that you're here, you're creating killer work and you'd still like to grow that relationship. It works a treat. Top of mind, top of heart.

These are just some of the ways you can help an end user get a true picture of you and everything you offer. You invest in going to the gym, buying new outfits for nights out and buying expensive drinks for social kudos – now it's time to invest time in getting professional kudos. Set aside a spring cleaning day and a regular time slot to stay on top of your online representation. Add, share, collaborate and update people with your progress. This isn't optional; it's essential.

The beauty of getting this done is that things like applying for jobs, networking and demonstrating your self-worth will become all that much easier, because you've finally got your shit in a row. (I know it's ducks in a row, but I always get my sayings wrong and I think it's more appropriate as you're not a four-year-old having a bath.) You will confidently opt in to putting yourself forward for things and showing off your talent – and you won't hold back the next time you do meet someone you respect or want to impress.

By following these simple steps and making yourself more approachable and accessible, you'll open up a whole new world of opportunities.

SEREENA ABBASSI

Worldwide Head of Culture & Inclusion at M&C Saatchi

▬

When was a time where you blagged your way through something and it paid off? How can people embrace the saying 'Blag now, worry later?'

'I've done loads of things where I haven't had tons of experience – even in my current career, I'd never done this in-house before. But I think when you're confident, confidence can get you really far. I feel like I'm always bringing my own personal experience to the table – and you can't question that, because it's mine. How I see it is – and I'm not a mum yet, but ... when you have your first baby, you have no bloody idea what you're doing but you do it, and hopefully you do it in a great way. We're all feeling our way through situations and you just need to have confidence. Your own personal experiences bring so much value – no one has walked through this world in the way you've walked through it. We're all unique. Even though we talk about businesses and organisations being a homogenous group of people, actually there's no such thing because we're all individuals.'

Getting the money you deserve can be tricky. What's the best money advice you could give to get what you're worth?

'It's really about doing your research. If you're going into a new role, do your research; there are loads of recruitment agencies that have listings on how much you should be earning. And even if you see that and you think "I'm worth more", then pitch yourself for more – but you have to give your reasons why. You have to be really clear what value you're bringing to the organisation – why you rather than someone else?'

Do you battle with imposter syndrome? If so, what advice would you give to people trying to overcome it?

'There was an incredible postcolonial theorist called Frantz Fanon who evolved the theory of "black double consciousness". If we were to translate this into gendered terms then we'd be talking about the "male gaze". Fanon explored the idea that I don't just perceive myself as "I", though I also perceive myself through the eyes of the majority. I think if I were to distil what imposter syndrome is, it's essentially about people seeing themselves through the eyes of another. So, if we no longer had to think about anyone else judging us – imagine it were only you in a room – who might we be, become in this world? It's through the process of feeling that we have eyes on us that makes us feel insecure and small. The way I combat this is that I choose not to allow my identity to be formed by anyone other than myself.'

FOUR

THE POWER OF NETWORKING

Now you've got a shit-hot online presence and you're getting used to sharing your work (even if it's only with your WhatsApp groups), it's time to start thinking about who's going to see it and how. You can invest all the time in the world in building a flawless profile, but if you've not got the connections in place for the right people to see it, you'll end up bitterly resenting the hours you've spent on it and you'll be left frustrated that your undeniable skill still hasn't been picked up.

Newsflash: everyone needs a distribution strategy, so don't think you're any different. It's time to start putting out the word.

When it comes to self-promotion, there are four words that it kills me inside to hear: 'I don't do networking'. It's literally like telling me you don't do take-aways on a hangover, or fancy Matthew McConaughey in *How to Lose a Guy in 10 Days*. Now, I do get it – the way that networking has been presented has been off-putting to the masses for decades. Middle-class white men, poorly fitting suits, cheap wine and chat that's dryer than the small talk you make with Uncle Nobhead at Christmas. Why on earth would you give up your free time for that? But the truth is that this is just one representation of *physical* networking – and it's one I hope is more of a dying breed than a common occurrence.

Networking has two sides: the physical and the digital. Although most people will only ever see physical networking as forced business encounters, I am here to tell you this doesn't have to be the case – and, dare I say it, physical networking can even be enjoyable. As for digital networking, I can't begin to tell you how lucky we are to be so connected to people all over the world. Thirty years ago, there was no internet, so all people could depend on was cold calling and word of mouth. How hard would that be! If you've never had to cold-call someone before, then lucky you; it's painful even for someone who can have a conversation with herself. Trying to build a rapport with someone who hasn't opted in and wasn't expecting your call is a struggle; and as for internet-less word of mouth, you definitely wouldn't be growing movements outside your local village hall very quickly. So yes, we are lucky to have the internet so readily accessible – whether you see it as a good thing all the time or not.

Now, I totally get this desire to 'digital detox' and go back to face-to-face communication, BUT there is no denying that there are a huge number of opportunities that can arise through the digital world – if you know how to seek them out.

The actual definition of networking is 'the exchange of information and ideas among people with a common profession or special interest'. How you choose to exchange that information is entirely up to you. We have to stop looking at networking as an old man's tech conference, and start thinking about all the amazingly incredible ways we can now connect with people – because in 2020 there are so many types of networking to get your head around and embrace.

METHODS OF NETWORKING IN 2020

* Chatting to like-minded people at industry events
* Scrolling through social media and sliding into DMs on Twitter, LinkedIn, the Dots, Instagram and Facebook, to name just a few
* Emailing people you admire all over the world
* Speaking on the phone to a long-lost friend who now works in a similar industry
* Exchanging stories at parties with people who run in similar networks
* Chatting to your colleagues at work
* Speaking over video calls to people on the other side of the world
* Watching live video streams of conferences you can't get to because you're in a different country
* Listening to podcasts and sharing them with people you want to impress
* Eating dinners and going for drinks with influencers in and out of your industry
* Catching up on webinars
* Midnight chats at McDonald's – you never know where they might lead
* And my personal favourite: handing out business cards in London parks (I even bagged a boyfriend out of that one – no lie)

The outdated rules of networking have shifted, and if you embrace at least one or two of the above in your spare time, I can guarantee you'll start to appreciate the power of networking. The irony is, you've probably already done or are doing many of the above. You've just got to stop viewing networking as something it's not. And here's how to do that ...

THE JOURNEY TO LOATHING NETWORKING — AND HOW TO GET BACK FROM IT

So why does networking get such a bad rep? Where did it go wrong? And where has the irrational hatred come from?

I've been observing the issue for a while now, and as someone who basks in social situations and loves meeting people, it's always baffled me that people find networking a battlefield. The most common feeling I've unearthed about networking is the 'fear of the unknown'. It's a situation you can't control or get out of easily but it could also have a significant impact on your reputation – good or bad. So, just like anything we fear, we choose to avoid it. We go through our formative years being told or telling ourselves that this type of activity isn't for us and never will be. We let labels like 'introvert' and 'extrovert' define whether we have the skills to do the task. We apply for jobs that have no requirements to attend networking-style events, and then as soon as we get into that job, we bury our head in the sand and hope the word is never mentioned. Society tells us who can and who can't do it, and we bow down and let it. But as with self-promotion, I want to change this perception – this completely unjustified view that not everyone can do it. And I'll begin by telling you this ...

MYTH-BUSTER ALERT: NO ONE IS BORN A NETWORKER

Not properly anyway. Sure, there are some people who have natural charisma and the ability to talk to new people, but the actual craft of networking is a *skill*. One that you have to understand, learn and put into practice relentlessly to become a 'master'.

I literally spent 18 months networking two or three times a week, every week, as well as working day in day out in people management – and I still wouldn't say I'm a master at it. And I definitely can't tell you that I don't cringe at the awkward things I've said (and continue to say) or get nervous about being rejected. So that's why it kills me when people say 'I'm not a networker' or 'You can do it because you're an extrovert'. I can do it because I put myself out there, out of my comfort zone, and I don't find excuses to limit my potential.

Let's be very clear again – it's not because I was born with it. Daniel Coyle has written an entire book about the fact that you're not born with talent. In *The Talent Code*, he explains that the people who succeed are the ones who are willing to look bad in order to get good – and this is true for networking too. Just like I referenced at the end of Chapter 1, we were all bad at sex at one point; it just depends how much you're willing to try in order to be better.

In his book, Coyle also explores how when we see people we admire or connect with doing things we deem unimaginable, we believe that we can do those things too. We are impressionable human beings, and just like I spent my entire life telling people I hated sparkling water and falafel because my dad always pulled a face whenever they were offered (which I later realised was not true, love them both now), many of you pull a face at networking because it's not something people around you do or claim to enjoy doing. But this doesn't mean you're not good at it or that you don't have the potential to be.

And while we're on the myth-busting train, I also want to challenge the 'it's not what you know, it's who you know' saying that's made so many small fishes (myself included) feel like they'll never catch a lucky break in their industry because they weren't born into the equivalent of the Beckham family. It's just not true. And the next time you hear it, choose to ignore it. I mean, I'm not going to spin some fairy-tale story that lots of people in the world who succeed aren't the children of wealthy celebrities, but I do want to restore some faith that just because you're not born into the world 'connected' doesn't mean you and your magnificently brilliant skills can't be connected in the future. I'm actually on a mission to change that saying to 'It's not who you know, it's who you are'.

Now, I realise I sound a bit like a doting parent sending their kid off to school for the first time, but it's so important to realise that while it might be breezier getting endless hook-ups from a friend of a friend, it's even more satisfying when you make that connection yourself based on *who you are*, all by yourself.

I come from a family of finance in Leeds: my mum is an accountant, my dad is in insurance, and if you don't know the North of England that well, it's hardly the creative capital of the world. And while my family were nothing but supportive throughout my childhood, the only connections they had were in the finance and accounting sector – and maths was never really my thing. When I realised I wanted to work in the creative world, I resented not having an uncle that worked at *Vice* magazine or a family friend that ran a marketing agency. But as soon as I got a job in the industry and jumped from one cool agency to the next, I never really thought it would be an issue again.

It was only when I uprooted my northern life and moved to London to naively join a start-up, Mattr.Media (taking on two roles – Senior Account Manager and New Business Manager), that the resentment started flooding back. There is often an assumption that if you're a chatty, outgoing person, new business and sales is a doddle; but from my experience that is absolutely not the case.

I was quickly brought down to earth by the reality of not having a single industry contact in London and needing to bring in a certain amount of money to hit business targets. This was by far the hardest and most challenging situation I had put myself in, in my entire working career. I was completely out of my depth and had a whole lot of weight on my shoulders – and there was a whole lot I was expected to deliver. Over the time I spent at the company, I did everything from cold calling and emailing, to networking three times a week, to running events and conducting interviews with brands we wanted to work with. Despite the immense challenges – and with a lot of hard work – my networking achievements included bringing in profitable new business, retaining clients, forging ongoing relationships, being provided with referrals, attracting sponsors and speakers for events, and gaining mentors, friends and, as I mentioned before, even a boyfriend.

It appeared the northern charm really did work down south. I had moved down to London unconnected, but within two years I became connected. Not by being handed a black book of contacts, but by grafting my arse off and putting myself out there. I was not born a networker – as I said, I don't believe anyone is – but I do hold my head up high as living proof that it's not about who you know, it's about who you are. I hope that by sharing this story and all the insights in this book, I can help you to stand out from whatever label you might have given yourself in the past – and see networking as the powerful tool that it really is.

Dave Kerpen sums up the importance of building meaningful connections in his book *The Art of People*:

> *Whether it's online or offline, the interactions and relationships with people around you, who these people are and what they are willing to do for you will determine how successful you will be. Have empty, weak relationships with the people around you and every challenge you face and every obstacle you encounter will feel like trying to push a*

boulder up a hill on your own. Cultivate authentic, mutually beneficial relationships built on trust, respect, and cooperation and getting the boulder up that hill will feel a lot easier thanks to the team of people pushing behind you.

Right, are you pumped and ready to move on to smashing networking?

No? I'm shocked.

Removes T-shirt with the slogan 'If you network, you'll get a boyfriend'.

Anyone can be a networker – we've just got to stop letting the stigma around the word and our lack of preparation be a barrier to sharing our personal stories. The more we process the skills we're growing and reflect on the incredible work we produce, the more natural it will feel telling people about our success. Whether it's in the pub or at an industry conference, being mentally prepared with the 'F*ck Being Humble' mantra will make it so much easier to seize the moment.

And for anyone who has ever dreaded networking, the next few pages take you through the key steps in overcoming that irrational state of FOSS (Fear Of Sounding Stupid) and making sure you gain from the next networking opportunity you find yourself in.

PREP IS KEY: PLANNING FOR NETWORKING OPPORTUNITIES

This isn't the first time I've gone on about the importance of preparation in this book, but when it comes to networking, the more you prepare, the less irrational fear you will take with you. Some of the key hesitations that people have about networking are:

* Forced chat with strangers
* Awkward silences

* Feeling vulnerable
* Having to sell yourself

I'm not going to lie, I don't think any of these anxieties ever truly disappear, but you can manage how much they bother you by putting in a bit of time on desk research and preparation. After all, when you go to a festival, you prepare in order to enhance your experience: planning your outfits, choosing the colour of glitter you'll wear, deciding what acts you can't miss, taking shoes that won't give you blisters and figuring out how you can disguise the greasiness of your hair on day four. The same goes for any type of networking situation: the more planning you do up front, the more enjoyable you'll find it. Treat it like a military operation and make sure you're getting the most from it. Here are my top 5 tips when it comes to networking:

1 WHAT'S YOUR AGENDA?

I've sat at many events that ended up being dull, watched Facebook Live videos I didn't learn a huge amount from and met with some very boring people – just because I didn't do my due diligence before I said yes. The most important thing you need to do before investing any time in networking is outline *why* you're doing it. What's your agenda, what's your overall goal, what type of people would you like to meet? And is this particular engagement going to help you achieve these things? That's not to say you can't drop someone a message or meet a friend for a coffee without having a key performance indicator attached, but if you network frequently, you'll want to treasure that precious time of yours.

2 DON'T KNOW WHAT TO TALK ABOUT?

A common issue that stops people from networking is not knowing what to talk about. We've already gone over knowing how to talk about your benefits and not just your features, but this is where your online stalking can truly come into play and help fuel endless conversation. Going to watch your idol speak at an event but worried about being star-struck? Spend some time online (preferably in advance, but I've also done this while sitting in the audience) reading up on their most recent news stories, where they've travelled, what they've been doing since their book launch, who they're hanging around with, what their competitors are doing, and what the general industry is saying about their topic of the event. Use your 24/7 access to the internet to your benefit. Something that I always try to do is find something that you mutually connect with and feed it into the conversation; people like to bond over a passion, so find something that shows you're on their wavelength. It's really important to also note that, although speaking to people for the first time can feel intimidating and nerve-wracking, you've done this before with everyone you have in your life. In the book *Do Improvise*, Robert Poyton talks about the fact that every conversation we have is improvised, you don't know what's coming next but you're always able to respond. Yet when it comes to networking situations, we tend to overthink everything that could go wrong rather than treating it in the same way as when we are having an unscripted conversation with friends. We have to stop building it up to be worse than it is; trust me you've got this.

3   SCARED ABOUT GOING ALONE?

The fear of networking alone is not something that should consume your mind. Being a loner at networking events is actually miles better than being with your friends or colleagues from work for a number of reasons. First, you're allowed to practise your pitch without your co-workers or mates making fun of you in the background. Second, you don't just sit talking to someone you already know about the prawn pasta they made at the weekend. And third, you can focus on yourself, you don't have to be dragged around by your partners-in-crime, and you can choose who to speak to and how long for. Embrace being a loner – it's so much better.

Top tip: If you still feel like you need a friend as a security blanket to support you, talk about your goals and big each other up when you meet someone you're trying to impress. You can rave about your best mate's killer awards cabinet until you feel comfortable to champion yourself. Find your Patsy to your Edina – and be each other's cheerleader.

4 WORRIED ABOUT SAYING THE WRONG THING?

With all the prep in the world, it's still easy to say the wrong thing, offend someone or create a tumbleweed big enough for Burning Man, but here's the thing – no one really cares. Your networking is going to go one of two ways: either it's going to go amazingly, and you'll connect and achieve your goals; or you'll mess up, you won't connect, it'll be forgotten about the next day and there are 7.3 billion other people in the world to work with instead. You've got to worry less about messing up, and just see any embarrassing moments as a funny story to tell down at the pub. I always say chill out, be more Bridget Jones – and have an empty glass of wine for when the chat dries up and you need an easy escape.

5 TRIED IT, HATED IT, VOWED NEVER TO DO IT AGAIN?

It's so easy to let a bad experience of one type of networking affect how you view getting involved, but it's really important to mix it up and try again. Networking is just having a conversation with someone (I've met contacts before on a plane to France), so try different mediums of connecting and put yourself in rooms with people you wouldn't normally hang out with. Keep trying different spaces, ask people where they go to find inspiration, set reminders on your calendar, sign up to newsletters and check *Time Out,* the Dots and Eventbrite religiously. Just like we go to new restaurant openings not knowing what to expect, the same goes for unfamiliar networking events.

I appreciate you can't always prepare for every type of networking or opportunity that might come your way – but the more you think about a personal goal for the event in advance, the easier it will be to hold the attention of the people you're trying to impress.

NETWORKING IN ACTION

Our biggest disappointment where networking is concerned is when we don't get what we want from it. But the reason we feel this way is because we set unbelievably high standards for ourselves and then beat ourselves up when we don't reach them. One of the best new business talks I ever attended was by Amy Jin, who worked in business development at Google and OpenTable. She had the most mesmerising presence, and everyone was hanging off her every word. At a point when I felt like I was failing at my new business role, she took that weight off my shoulders by stressing that it isn't about conquering the world in one day and it's unrealistic to set that sort of standard. The best way to keep your momentum is to identify mini-milestones that will help you to reach your larger goals.

It's common sense, really. If you wanted to run a marathon for the first time, you wouldn't go straight out and try a 26-mile run – you'd work up to it and pace yourself. When you're matching with people on dating apps, the first question you ask isn't 'Can we be boyfriend and girlfriend?' (although I kind of wish that worked) – instead you build up to it by exchanging information until something clicks. And when you're a writer, you sure as hell don't publish the first words you ever put to paper – you write, it gets edited, you write more, it gets edited even more, and then finally it's ready to share with the rest of the world. The same goes for networking. As I said, it's a skill – and there is an art to it – but even the best networkers are unlikely to convert a lead first time round.

So what are 'mini-milestones', and how do they relate to networking? Well, there could be a number of different goals that you set and aim to reach over a certain period of time – ranging from getting a response to a message, to someone giving you their personal contact details, to signing up to a newsletter or being introduced to a connection. All of these interactions will send you in the right direction towards building longer-term relationships. And they will help you to identify your progress, even though they are small steps.

So do yourself a favour, and when you plan your agenda, map out your mini-milestones and have everything you need in order to embrace your smaller wins.

LISTEN FIRST, SELL LATER

If you pitch your story too early, you could take yourself out of the running because you didn't take the time to listen to what impresses the person in front of you. Ask as many questions as possible, and at the right moment (which is usually towards the end of the conversation) present yourself and your offering. This is particularly helpful if you don't class yourself as a conversation-hogger and limelight-holder: people love talking about themselves, so let them – and show how good a listener you are.

DON'T BE TOO FUSSY

At school, the cool kids get picked for the sports teams first, but try to avoid investing your time in only higher-profile people. Sure, it's good to have a target, but you'd be surprised how rubbing shoulders with people who are more junior can open doors quicker for you. Most likely because they'll be more on your wavelength, have more time and won't palm you off onto their PA. Even if it's not with the person you were hoping to speak to, they might be able to connect you to someone completely new. The titles people have on their name badges and bios aren't always all they have to offer. Be open-minded, speak to everyone and don't always chase the hero of the show.

CONVERSATION STARTERS

A man walked into a bar and said 'ouch' has been my go-to joke for 27 years, but sometimes – just sometimes – even that doesn't work to break the ice. So what does? Well, I'll be honest, it's not much more inventive than asking politely to join a conversation (which works better if you're a loner – you get the sympathy vote). Here are a few different ways to open and steer a conversation:

* 'Did you come alone too?'
* 'Who are you here to hear from?'
* 'Have you been to these events before?'
* 'Have you heard this speaker before?'

* 'Do you work in the industry?'
* 'I love the work your company produces – what are you currently working on?'

BE VULNERABLE

People like people they can connect with. I know that's an obvious statement, but it's important to remember that how you portray yourself, both online and offline, will be how people judge you. When I say 'be vulnerable', I don't mean offloading your feelings about your recent break-up on a stranger, but sharing professional challenges you might be going through and connecting with people through empathy can be a great way to build honest long-term relationships. No one wants a human megaphone in their face reeling off all your most amazing achievements, so share your personal side and make a real connection.

> Top tip: Remember not to be too self-deprecating. It's a British commonality that often makes people feel uncomfortable, particularly if they don't know you well enough to provide a counterargument.

HAVE A TROJAN HORSE READY

A bit like setting your mini-milestones, sometimes the thing you ask for when connecting isn't what you really want from them, but it will help you get on their radar. Something I've previously done is interview brand leaders with interesting back stories, the thought process being that I get to ask them questions about their journey to date, what's gone well and what they've struggled with – and, in doing so, I'm able to understand their weak spots and offer the right solution to them in the future. The same applies if you want someone to speak at an event you're running. Rather than asking them the first time you meet, you might give them a complimentary ticket to something you're hosting so they can be involved in the process. Try to give them multiple options so they don't have a reason to say no.

GIVE THEM SOMETHING IN RETURN

Something I always encourage people to do is to think about how you can add value to someone else, even if it doesn't immediately help you reach your goals. As I mentioned, it's unusual that you'll get exactly what you're looking for the first time you meet, but rather than throwing your toys out of the pram, think about how you can build that relationship for the future. Could you introduce them to someone of benefit, share a relevant book or podcast, or even invite them to the next event you go to? Good things happen to those who help selflessly (even if there is a hidden motive!).

MAKE YOURSELF APPROACHABLE

Put your phone in your pocket and make that smile of yours noticeable (but not in a creepy, OTT way). Look up, try to catch people's attention, let them know you're in the room and present. When you do start speaking to them, make eye contact, nod regularly and stay neutral if they say something you don't necessarily agree with. Remember, a first meet with someone is usually a snapshot of them, so unless they've read this book, they probably struggle with networking too and don't always present themselves in the best way. Try to avoid your eyes wandering, and give that person the undivided attention they deserve.

SEIZE THE MOMENT

One of my favourite networking stories took place at a SheSays event (a series set up to champion females in the advertising industry). The event host was having technical issues, and they asked the audience if there was anyone who was working on a project that they wanted to share with the group. I watched a couple of women confidently raise their hands, felt the adrenaline rush through me, palms at peak sweatiness, and stood up to share my recently formed platform, F*ck Being Humble. When I say 'recent', I literally mean three weeks old. Following Amy Jin's mini-milestones advice, I asked for two things from the audience: to follow the Instagram account, and if anyone knew of free event space in London. In that one announcement, I got about 70 new followers and made 'F*ck Being Humble' official. I will never forget the moment – and to all the women who were in that room and who still support the platform, thank you.

Every networking scenario you're in, find a way to seize the moment and get something back for giving your personal time. It doesn't have to be anything as major (or terrifying) as standing up in front of a crowd – it could be just talking to one new person at each event.

FORGET ABOUT REJECTION

I can't tell you how many times I've heard someone say 'I was going to stand up but then I bottled it' for no reason other than they were worried that what they were going to say wouldn't be well received. But this fear of rejection is very often unjustified – and as we mentioned before, it's irrational. One of my favourite TED Talks is '100 days of rejection', in which Jia Jiang describes setting himself 100 tasks that would result in rejection: from asking Krispy Kreme for five donuts in the colours and shape of the Olympic rings, to ordering a burger and asking not to pay for the food. Why? All so he could get over this fear of rejection. The idea went so well, he turned it into 'Rejection Therapy' and has since written a book about it!

Rejection is a psychological barrier that can be avoided, so don't let the voices in your head hold you back from putting yourself out there – and practise being turned down. It really isn't as bad as it seems. When you feel yourself letting the fear of rejection seep through, remind yourself 'F*ck being humble, I deserve this moment'.

REMEMBER THAT YOU WILL COMPLEMENT S AND THAT YOU DON'T TO DO IT ALL.

LEYYA SATTAR AND ROSHNI GOYATE, FOUNDERS OF THE OTHER BOX

STRENGTHS
MEBODY ELSE'S
AVE TO BE ABLE

REMOTE NETWORKING

To rewind to my earlier point of at one time being an unconnected person in the creative industries, I need and want to stress that nearly all of the connections I have made – the people I worked with on new business opportunities, those I had speak on my panels, those who invited me to speak on their panels and any press I have received – were not fostered through a mate from school hooking me up or only through face-to-face meetings. I've built a good percentage of my network through digital platforms, because the internet is our saviour and we'd be seriously lost without it. While we're all busy moaning about social media being the sole reason for our insecurities and loss of time, we seem to forget that *we control what we consume*. We can use our digital access to further our knowledge, connections and position simply by being tactical and inquisitive anywhere in the world. We just need to change our interaction with social media to focus on upskilling and broadening our awareness instead of fat-shaming and inducing unwanted stress.

RESEARCH DOESN'T HAVE TO INVOLVE BOOKS

Although I pride myself on being a regular networker, there are many times where physical networking just doesn't fit into my schedule. But somehow, no matter how busy I am, I always find time for my daily social scrolling. I search, follow, explore and make note of people who catch my eye who could be cool to work with or champion. Often, the best way to make sure they don't slip through the net is by sending them a message introducing yourself, or commenting on a post and expressing your interest in their work. Remember, many of our relationships start in the digital world through a simple 'like'. I did this recently when an employee from the *Guardian* added me on LinkedIn and hadn't immediately messaged. I sent her a short message updating her on *F*ck Being Humble*, which led to a phone call and one week later I was at their office speaking to their internal teams about hosting a talk. Refocus how much time you spend aimlessly scrolling and put your time to good use by actually connecting with people – it's incredible how lost you'll get in the endless sea of inspiration.

PUT YOURSELF ON A PLATTER

Similar to my previous advice about sending contacts your latest relevant work updates, do the same with people and businesses you admire and would like to be part of. Lecture in Progress, a platform set up by the magazine *It's Nice That*, is a space to inspire future generations on the path to success in the creative industries. I always rated their content and aspired to one day be featured on the podcast, so rather than wait for them to approach me, I contacted them. I introduced myself, told them what I do and what I felt I could offer, and on this (rare) occasion they'd actually heard of me and had planned to invite me to feature on the series anyway. The next thing I knew I was recording my first-ever podcast in my living room with their content creator. Don't wait to be found – put yourself on a platter and make yourself so appealing they can't miss out.

LOCATION DOESN'T NEED TO BE A BARRIER

Companies do international business all the time digitally, but when it comes to networking we claim that our location is the dictator of success. WRONG. It's really, really not. For as long as we have image-sharing, messaging and video-recording capabilities, we can tell our stories via YouTube, Twitter, Instagram, LinkedIn and Facebook overnight, all of which stay online for you to later share with others who want to see examples of your work. If you are based outside your country's or industry's 'hubs', think about how you can create a disruption to the current content in that space – or who you might be able to collaborate with that does have a presence in the space you want to excel in.

FIND YOUR ALLIES

A little like having a Patsy to your Edina at networking events, find your online allies. Whether it's a share, an introduction or co-creation, build a community of supporters that will help spread your message. A simple way I did this for my event series is by encouraging designers to create artwork to summarise the theme of the evening; they very often shared the artwork ahead of the event, raising awareness of not only their talent but their affiliation with the platform. But you can also be more tactical in finding your cheerleaders and look for people who have a high reach and existing reputation in the industry. If you're questioning why they would care, it's up to you to do your research (aka social stalking) to find a personal connection with them – maybe even finding something they are struggling with and offering up your support. An ally is about mutual backing; don't assume you'll get anything for free in this world.

So whether you're networking at a panel event in central London or remote net-working from a coffee shop in Manchester, you now have a list of ways to begin to utilise your reach and build your network.

The truth is, you control how 'connected' you are, and it's your responsibility to put yourself out there. As we've discussed, you can wait for the opportunities to come to you, or you can go out and get them. The excuse that you don't *know* people is no longer good enough. Networking involves so many different types of activities, you just have to keep trying until you find the ones you connect with the most!

THE FOLLOW-UP

The follow-up to networking can be long, hard work and not very rewarding. But two pieces of advice I'll give to you are: don't take anything personally, and be persistent. My boyfriend often jokes that my tombstone will read 'Stefanie Sword-Williams – Fucking relentless' for many reasons, the main one being that I don't give up easily. I can't say that's always been the case or that I haven't sulked when I sent an epic follow-up email and the marketing director of a global brand didn't reply, but what I have learned is to be a realist. People have lives that don't revolve around you, and you can't let their lack of an instant response be a deterrent to your plans. If anything, use it as a driving force to show them what an amazing opportunity they missed out on by not getting back to you.

The following list are my dos and don'ts when it comes to making sure you continue your relationship past your initial meet:

DO: STAY IN TOUCH WITH THE CONVERSATION ON SOCIALS

Most networking occasions are documented on social media, and through images, tweets and hashtags you can find people, add them, follow them and send them a message introducing yourself. It doesn't have to be long, it just needs to be a reminder of how and where you met; and if you had a personal connection, then share that too. And I'm not just talking about the guest speakers, I'm talking about the people in the audience. It doesn't have to be stalkerish – you can just drop them a note to say, 'Saw you attended the event, it was so great, wasn't it? Would have been good to connect but hopefully see you at the next one!' Simple and not intense, and that person will now remember you as someone who has a similar interest to them and might be worth considering for future engagements.

DON'T: <u>**EXPECT THEM TO FIND YOU**</u>

At the end of D&AD Festival (a global creative industry event full of inspirational TED-style talks and showcases of award-winning work), I was so in awe after hearing Patrick Collister, then creative lead at Google, that I needed to find a way to connect with him. So I approached him at the end of his talk, told him how inspired I was and asked if he'd be my mentor. Definitely one of my braver moments. I got his business card, emailed him within 24 hours of meeting him, and the next week I was at Google's head offices looking out over the London skyline. But would he have found me otherwise? Would he have searched for my profile on LinkedIn and offered to give his time to help further my career? Of course he wouldn't. How can you expect people to find you and offer you what you need in life if you don't make them aware of it?

I asked for a mentor that day, but it could have been an introduction to another connection or even a new job.

And if I hadn't asked that day, I wouldn't have got anything. But always remember that sometimes you can have a great conversation with someone and then it goes nowhere – not because it didn't have the potential to, but because there wasn't enough action in the follow-up. So make it your mission to follow up on all encounters.

DO: EMAIL FAST AND MAKE IT PERSONAL

The sooner you can email the person the better, as the fresher you are in their memory, the more likely they'll remember and prioritise you. I know it can feel like a total chore when you've already got an overflowing inbox, but if you want to ensure they're left with a positive impression of you, showing that you're eager to connect is always going to put you at the front of their mind. And if you know you're going to have a crazy week, set a calendar reminder to do it over the weekend so you don't forget!

There are four things to consider when crafting a killer follow-up email:

1   *Introduce and connect.* Include your name, your role and your reason for emailing in the first sentence. This is your time to hook them in and cut through.
2   *Qualify yourself.* Based on your perfectly curated online platforms (see Chapter 3), include a link – whether it's to a website or LinkedIn profile – so that they can qualify you and immediately see your work.
3   *Leave them with something memorable.* Mention something you've done in relation to your request that indicates how seriously you take your work. An example of this is when I sent my cover note to an employer, and I included that I'd danced with Lorraine Kelly on a

set to help keep things moving and helped break the ice on a photoshoot – not that this was necessarily my role, but it demonstrated that I'll go the extra mile when I need to. What have you done in your career that demonstrates your dedication?

4. *Always propose an action.* Please, please, whatever you do – do not end that email passively. Suggest a meeting, say you'll follow up in a couple of days, ask to set up a call. Give them something they feel they need to reply to. Don't let your email fall into the ether because you ended it with 'Look forward to hearing from you'. You might as well end it with 'Don't worry about replying if you're busy'.

DON'T: <u>ASK FOR THEIR PERMISSION</u>

We very easily suffer from imposter syndrome in our working environment, and it's even more prevalent when we're reaching out for something or connecting with people more senior to us. When I worked at a start-up that was going through a growth period, we worked with Adam Graham, Founder of Gray Matters, a business development consultancy, who explained the importance of talking to people you want to impress as if you are on a similar level to them. As a start-up company, we always recognised that we were very often the least well-known option in the mix, and even if it was just subconsciously, it would affect how we presented ourselves and who we felt confident enough to be in a room with. What Adam did was give us a much-needed confidence booster: telling us that we shouldn't ask for people's permission. Instead, we should speak to them like we'd earned our place in the conversation. So if you catch yourself slipping into Oliver Twist–esque begging, *stop* – and use a more positive phrase instead. The following list gives you some common things people say when they're not confident in their position, and an example of how you can sound more convincing:

* I'd be honoured if you'd consider me ... > I can see you value craft, which is great, because it's something I pride myself on ...
* Please could you consider ... > It would be a great opportunity ...
* I'd be so grateful for your time ... > I'm speaking to leaders in this field ...

Also, let's face it, the only person you'd really say 'honoured' and 'grateful' to is if you were asking the Queen to come over for afternoon tea.

DO: <u>BE PERSISTENT WITH YOUR MESSAGING</u>

I know how painful it can be to not get the desired response – or any response at all – when you really want to connect with someone. But sadly, that's life: we all have our own stuff going on, and the stars don't always align when you need them to. But don't give up after just one email; after all, we don't give up on friends or family when they don't return our call the first time round, do we?! I do get that it's hard not to feel like you're coming across as pushy, so I like to share some advice I learned from a colleague – the simple 'three message' rule:

1   *The introduction*. The first email, detailing who you are, what you do and what you're requesting from them. With, of course, a proposed action.

2   *The polite follow-up.* The second email is about checking they received the original email, and referring back to your request as a reminder.

3   *The final chance.* Still remaining polite, this is your final email before you give up. You can say something like 'I wanted to follow up one final time to see if this was of interest to you. If not, I'll reconnect with you in the coming months.'

The third email is the magic game changer – trust me. The reason it works so well is it creates scarcity, communicating that you and what you're offering is no longer going to be available if they don't seize this opportunity. And if they don't seize the opportunity, then put them on a separate contact list or in a special folder and set reminders to follow up in six months' time. Don't let them go *too* quickly!

Top tip: Sometimes it's worth mixing it up and calling rather than sending follow-up emails. You never know, they might not have received your first email or they might let on more information that you can't always gauge in a digital message.

DON'T: <u>CUT OFF A CONTACT BECAUSE THEY DIDN'T FALL AT YOUR FEET THE FIRST TIME ROUND</u>

It's so easy to want to write someone off, especially if they've ignored three emails in a row, but I beg you: don't dismiss them all together. Yes, it's rude to blank someone that many times, but if you're not top priority in that person's life, then you've got to learn not to take it personally. Before starting my old job, I'd actually applied for a role there two years previously but nothing came of it. As a follow-up to my application, I'd contacted the managing director of the company on LinkedIn to ask when they'd be reviewing, and he'd replied to say they'd do so in the coming weeks – and then I never heard back. I could have sulked and told myself I clearly wasn't good enough, or decided to never work for them out of pride, but they were a company I'd always wanted to work at and I knew I could offer them something more. So two years later, I reconnected with him, detailed what I'd been doing since I'd reached out, and one week later I'd got a job that hadn't even been advertised.

We have this unwritten ambition that by the time we're 30 we'll have a high-flying job, a marriage and be a home-owner, but the reality is that everything doesn't always fall into place in the timelines we imagined aged 14. Much as I didn't have an automatic hub of brands I could ask to work with when I moved down to London to work in new business, sometimes the contacts we need to impact our lives aren't always standing on our doorstep waiting to help. Don't let the setbacks be a permanent tattoo of failure – have faith that, one day, that contact will help you if you make yourself regularly known and top of mind.

DO: **<u>MAKE IT AN ONGOING RELATIONSHIP</u>**

I mentioned the Trojan horse theory earlier, but the best way to maximise a new connection is to build a genuine relation-ship. Put simply: invest in them like you would a friend. One of my favourite stories is about a guy who wanted to gain business with Lloyds Bank, so every two or three months he would visit their office two hours away, take them for lunch and travel home with nothing in return. He did this for sev-eral years, and eventually they appointed his company as the lead creative agency, with a substantial spend attached to it. He sold up and moved on after that – but Jesus, that's commitment. During that time he was able to show himself to be a credible, reliable and talented resource. He earned his stripes and (eventually) reaped the rewards.

For many of us, regular lunches or dinners aren't going to be affordable, but other ways we build relationships with people can be low-cost but high-value. When Shannie Mears, Co-Founder of creative agency The Elephant Room and Founder of Girls Let's Talk, first worked in an advertising agency, she noticed that the people surrounding her didn't have a broad understanding of urban culture, so she decided to circulate a weekly email – the 'Urban Lowdown' – sharing rising talent, interesting communities, movements, podcasts, upcoming events and anything that could inspire her colleagues in a different way. By regularly sharing these insights, Shannie carved out a name for herself and built a reputation of having great cultural awareness. Being – and staying – remembered is key to building networks, and even if it's just regular sharing, liking and commenting on digital posts, showing that you support that person in some shape or form will help an ongoing relationship.

DON'T: MAKE IT OBVIOUS YOU'RE ONLY AFTER ONE THING (AKA THE 'BOOTY CALL')

When we don't get what we want immediately, we often lose interest in that source; and trust me when I say, *it shows*. If you're someone who only ever reaches out when there's something in it for you, it will become very clear what your agenda is. It's important to have a consistent and well-rounded approach, and to use the examples above to build an ongoing relationship. Just like we see through time-wasters, people see through self-seekers too.

As you can probably tell, I'm pretty passionate about networking ... the main reason being it has dramatically changed the life of little old northern me. It is not something that should be dictated by age, class, gender or hierarchy; it is all about seeking out long-term relationships of mutual benefit. It's very easy to feel alone – whether you're employed, freelance, running your own business, or even just because you don't have all your close friends around you.

You never know when having or supporting a contact could change your life, so be open to getting involved – and make networking as much a priority as you do the other self-improvement activities in your life.

SHANICE MEARS

The Elephant Room
& Founder of Girls let's talk

——

What's one of your best attributes and how did you figure it out?

'Figuring out your best attribute is an ongoing work-in-progress. There are things that I know I'm good at, like communicating with people, understanding an idea and figuring out who to onboard to make sure it gets executed properly; but then at the same time they're not always things you can put down on a piece of paper, or if you don't have the right network or opportunity you can't always show them to others. For me it's about asking "How do I come across effectively?" but also "How do I know it's working?" I'm always in constant conversation with people – getting opinions on whether I'm taking the right approach – and I think always getting another person's opinion is something that I value and a way I can know whatever I'm doing is working.'

What's your top trick to be remembered for what you do; how do you position yourself in a unique way?

'I don't just build relationships so that my network can be amazing – I build relationships thinking, "What can I offer you in return for whatever I'm gaining?" People remember me for being genuine; it's not about me trying to get something from them, it's about how we can build something together, so anything I see that I think would be good for someone I'll pass on or I'll put in the group chat. That's why I created The Guestlist – I would see things all the time and think "How can I build a community where everyone gets an in?" It's now around 1,000 people and counting, and everyone's sharing opportunities, and that's why people remember me because I'm not just in it to build something for myself, I'm wanting to build something for everyone else, too.'

Getting the money you deserve can be tricky. What's the best money advice you could give to get what you're worth?
'Everything I do is about value exchange, and I don't look at money as the end goal. It's very important in terms of mindset to look at both short-term goals and long-term goals financially, and whatever moves you're making, asking what that means for you and how you achieve that. I think a lot of the time we get caught up in the idea of getting paid, but to be honest I would much rather not get paid for something and build an incredible network so that I've got that network for the next job and know I can get paid for anything. For me, I don't get paid to sit at 10 Downing Street, but that gives me credibility, and the people I'm in the room with have a lot of money, so I now understand how to get sponsors for things, or where to go for funding because I have a great network – I don't necessarily get paid to sit on that board but I know that my time will eventually be paid for. I think the question is: What do you truly value and what are you doing the work for?'

FIVE

KNOWING YOUR SELF-WORTH

was at the pub with two friends recently, and my mate Claire (who's Australian) asked us, 'What's your favourite physical thing about yourself?' With Hannah and I being the cynical Brits we are, we looked puzzled and were unusually lost for words. It's not really a question you're prepared for when you've spent so long criticising your ironing-board chest and cellulite-covered legs. You're usually ready to list all the personal improvements you'd like to make – not admire the things you've got.

There are things that I like about my visual appearance, but to state the one thing I loved most about myself was quite a challenge. We cackled as we said things like our necks, the length of our arms and our bushy hair, but all three of us could easily identify all the amazing things about each other that we didn't see in ourselves. (Granted, the rosé helped the circle of positivity – but nonetheless it was totally genuine.)

What that night made me realise was that it's not just our physical appearances that we don't spend enough time appreciating, it's our professional abilities too. I've had endless conversations with friends who have struggled to bring to life their most impressive achievements because, when your confidence is low and you're not used to self-reflection, you forget to acknowledge the incredible things you do or have done so far. And, let's face it, it's rare that your bosses or colleagues will instigate a support circle of praise, so it's no wonder we're not as vocal about our technical drawing skills as we are about our abnormally long eyelashes (and most of us Brits aren't even good at bragging about those). Just like having good self-awareness can help you spot when you're being an irrational diva, having a true understanding of what your best qualities and professional achievements are will help you to self-promote, comfortably and confidently.

I get asked a lot: How do you figure out your self-worth? How do you know how much you deserve or whether you've earned the right to be where you are? If you're asking these questions, you are 100 per cent human. We all struggle to know our worth from time to time. But as I've got older, developed more skills and gained further experience, I've learned to recognise that the more I **accept** that I'm getting better and take **pride** in my achievements, the higher I value myself.

The reason I highlight acceptance and pride is because I believe they are secret weapons in overcoming that godawful imposter syndrome that we fight off on a daily basis. And during reviews and money negotiations, they are what will drive you to get the reward that you deserve.

We'll get on to money chat in the next chapter, but the first step to understanding your self-worth is believing in your talent – and here's how to do it ...

ACCEPT THAT YOU'RE ACTUALLY GOOD AT YOUR JOB

We spend our lives longing for validation and praise, but very often when we receive it, we just don't know how to accept it. Whether it's a result of previous bad relationships, or bosses never commending your hard work, or the very fact you don't believe in yourself, we all regularly downplay our abilities to the point where we're unable to realise that we are worthy of where we've got to today. FYI, this is not okay, and it is highly detrimental to your future.

When people tell you you've done a good job, accept it. When people say you're good with people, accept it. When people say you're a valued team member, accept it. People don't have to say these things to you (and in some cases, it might actually pain them to do so!), so stop denying yourself the recognition and learn to accept that you are good at your job. Each year you will be improving, and each year you will receive some type of praise that indicates you've done a good job. That praise might not always be verbal or from the people you really want to hear it from, but things like repeat business, increased engagement and general business growth are all things that you can identify and accept are to do with *you*.

I've said it before but I'll say it again: make sure you document all the little and big wins so you can reference them when you need a reminder. The sooner you accept that your skills are valuable, the more self-confidence you'll have to demand what you're worth.

TAKE PRIDE IN WHAT YOU DO

I often get pulled up for talking about work in social situations, but I've realised that I do this because I'm proud of the work I do, and I want to share it. In opening that dialogue, discussing it with others and displaying my passion, I am recognising the many ways that I'm growing both in terms of skills and as a person. The more we take pride in our work, the more likely we are to share and reflect on our achievements. By keeping work 'at work', we don't always allow ourselves the headspace to acknowledge our wins, be they big or small.

So the next time you're proud of a work achievement, share it with someone *not at work*. Talk them through why you're proud of it, what you contributed to the process and how you've grown from it, and accept the well-deserved praise you'll get. Try to make it a habit: find someone who really supports you and wants to listen, as very often they can help identify things you hadn't even thought of – thus helping you to be even more accepting of your talent. And enjoy the emotion you feel when you acknowledge your success, whether it's pure excitement, or that tingly feeling you get just before your eyes start to well up, or just the satisfaction of feeling that little bit more complete. You really *are* doing a good job, so take it in your stride.

One of the hardest and saddest things I see is when women, in particular, have spent 20 years in their role and are still battling imposter syndrome. Somewhere along their journey, they were made to think they weren't worthy of their role or their place in the industry. But when you accept and take pride in what you do, you show other people that you do deserve to be there. We have to stop questioning whether we've done enough to earn our place and start thinking about how showing off our success can help us – but also others. Maybe an article you wrote encourages someone to quit their day job and follow their dreams. Maybe a photo you shared helps someone else secure a project they are pitching for. Maybe an anecdote you tell helps another person with a mental health issue. By embracing your self-worth, and bringing it to the surface, you can also help others.

I'm trying my hardest not to round this off with a motivational Beyoncé lyric, but ultimately the sooner you believe in yourself and accept that you're good at your job and you have talent worth acknowledging, the easier it will be to convince others you're worth the investment.

We have to stop letting our doubts overtake what we can achieve.

SPEAK TO OTHERS: THE IMPORTANCE OF MENTORS

Before I started 'F*ck Being Humble', I always told myself that one day I'd like to be a mentor. I knew I'd like to find ways to help people – particularly as I never felt like I had that one person always looking out for me in the industry. But as I reflect on my career (and my personal life), I've had lots of mentors. They may not have been icons in my industry, but I've always had parents, friends, colleagues, bosses, boyfriends and teachers that I could open up to about my career and ask questions when needed.

I can be terrible at making my mind up, and I very often look for guidance from people whose opinions I respect the most. Sometimes I take their advice, and sometimes I do exactly what I intended to do before I spoke to them. Annoying for them? Maybe! But the more you ask people for support and advice, the more rounded your opinions, decision-making and life choices will be. Here are a few top tips on how to get the most from mentors:

• <u>KILL THEM WITH FLATTERY</u>

A common issue I often hear is 'I don't know where to find a mentor'. Just as I explained in previous chapters, connections (aka potential mentors) are everywhere – you just have to seek them out. The reality is, people love being asked to be mentors, because it means their opinion is respected, so if there is someone you particularly admire ... JUST GO AHEAD AND ASK THEM. You don't need to know them, and nor do you even have to be in the same country or time zone. Use things like LinkedIn, industry events or social media messaging to open the conversation.

• TRY HAVING MULTIPLE MENTORS

Olivia Crooks, an account manager at Spotify, spoke at one of my first events about the power of mentors – and her advice was 'don't just stop at just one'. As a black female navigating her way through the world of advertising, she had three different mentors: a white, experienced male mentor who was able to teach her how to climb the ladder and ask for more money; a black female mentor within the industry who shared her experiences of overcoming similar barriers; and a female mentor outside her industry who gave her 'reality check' feedback. By having these three different influences in her life, Olivia could make considered and tactical decisions about her career and benefit from the wisdom of three minds instead of just one.

• DON'T PUT TOO MUCH PRESSURE ON THEM

When I asked Olivia how she managed to convince three people to mentor her, she said, 'They often don't know they're my mentors!' Rather than put a label on the relationship, or advertise any sort of expectation, Olivia just reaches out to these individuals as and when she's looking for guidance. As much as people are willing to support you, they also have lives of their own to manage, so it's worth considering how you pitch the parameters of the relationship – dependant on the amount of time you need from someone. If you'd like to have a weekly phone call, it's probably important you state that early on, but if you just plan to email them every few months as and when something pops up, you don't necessarily need to label the relationship as 'mentorship', especially if you're concerned their time might be limited.

• WHAT THEY SAY ISN'T GOSPEL

There is no disputing that having mentors can benefit your decision-making and provide alternative viewpoints, but it is really important that you only follow the advice you feel connects most with you. A mentor is there to guide you, but what they say isn't gospel and you shouldn't feel you have to carry out everything they advise. Stay true to yourself, and use mentors as a source to help inform your decisions – not dictate your life.

• MENTORS DON'T HAVE TO BE ICONS

Not every mentor you have will have the same status as Will Smith or Tyler, The Creator, and quite frankly that's not a bad thing. Mentors can be in a similar age group and role and even have the same amount of experience as you, and you can still learn from them. There are also a lot of companies doing 'reverse mentoring', which is where a junior member of staff advises someone senior. The generations coming up are most likely going to be able to teach us how we could be doing things more efficiently or even how to stay more culturally relevant, so don't get hung up on your mentor being a icon in the field – and seek out anyone who can benefit your weak spots.

Mentors are people who want to see you do well whatever their age, status or seniority. Go to the people you admire, and fangirl (or fanboy) them the same way you would if you were meeting Sean Paul for the first time. Let them help you improve your weaknesses, map out your world domination and be there for you when it comes to celebrating your successes.

Now, stop being a martyr, and go find a mentor.

DON'T BE A ONE-HIT WONDER

When it comes to being noticed as a credible talent, it's really important to build your reputation all year round, instead of two days before your annual review. I always found it really funny when people I worked with would 'buck up their ideas' and put in that extra effort in the few weeks before the company was about to make a decision on the bonus payout – almost like our bosses wouldn't see right through it! It was like watching a kid stop crying as they hear the ice cream van jingle coming down their road.

Opportunities can arise at any time, so reputation-building should be a constant task you're always aware of and always actively looking to do. By only self-promoting two weeks before you realise your freelance job is about to be up, you'll open yourself up to new opportunities solely at that point in time.

We've talked about the importance of having your online portfolio updated and sharing your work, but here are some other areas to consider when building that street cred of yours ...

BE A SELF-INITIATED VALUE-ADDER

Most companies and clients will look for self-initiators that they don't need to hand-hold to add value to their business. Just as Shannie Mears offered up her intel, you could be proactively sharing articles you read, podcasts you've listened to, films you've watched, free tickets you can pass on and so on. And even if you're not directly involved in a project at work and you felt you should have been, don't just sulk in the corner cursing them – instead, send them anything useful they could benefit from so they can see you have a passion and interest in the topic. It's much better to show that you are actively engaged in the industry than be someone who rarely speaks up and only appears to be there out of necessity.

YOU ARE MORE THAN YOUR TITLE

I've always been someone who seeks out companies that don't have a strict hierarchy and don't pigeonhole you into a specific role, as this means that I can get involved in various parts of the business without feeling I need to seek out permission. I always admired how my old account manager Kat wouldn't just write amazing briefs for projects, she'd also share cultural and creative references to help guide the creative teams. She didn't have to do that and it wasn't expected of her, but she knew everything about runway trends, restaurant launches and makeup collabs, and she wasn't going to let her job title get in the way of positively influencing a brief or new opportunities for the company. And when she could see that her next linear step was to become an Account Director (something she'd always feared becoming as the role became less hands-on and actually less fun), she realised she didn't want to follow suit. Instead she pitched an entirely new role of 'Head of Culture', an uncommon title in the ad industry, but one that would reflect her interests and also be a valuable addition to the company. Because of the reputation she had built and the irreplaceable asset she had become, the company accepted her proposal within 24 hours and she continues to add cultural insights to every project she can. Don't let your role limit your potential; bring to work the additional knowledge you have and make it available to the right people.

Another reason not to let labels limit you is that often people have ready-made preconceptions of what your job title means. So you tell them you're a PR assistant, but what they don't see is everything you might do to be good at that role, or what you do outside your day job that contributes towards your reputation. A job title can place restrictions on what people think of you and your abilities, so it's up to you to speak up.

Focus on making people aware of exactly what it takes to be exceptional at your job, show them the extra work that you do and explain your point of difference to the next person who asks you, 'What do you do?' Don't be afraid to speak up about your side hustles and passion projects either, the skills you grow externally could help paint a much more vivid picture of who you are. If I walked into rooms only ever saying I was an Account Director, people wouldn't know that I public-speak, run events, curate content for social media or mentor rising talent, as none of this is expected in my day job title.

PUT YOURSELF OUT OF YOUR COMFORT ZONE

Whether it's socially or professionally, taking part in activities that you wouldn't normally be expected to do or want to do is a great way to build your reputation. Public speaking, pottery classes, learning Mandarin or even joining a rowing club are all things that could help to showcase your personality and outlook. Pottery-making could put you on the map as someone who understands materials and their form; and rowing sessions might mean you can help a colleague who is working on an outdoor-sportswear brief. The key is to try new things and share them with others, as you never know when someone might need expertise in that space and how you might be able to support them.

DON'T BE UNAPPROACHABLE

I know it sounds obvious, but very often decisions are based on you being a likeable person. Skills can be trained up, but the wrong attitude or energy is something you can't force down people's throats. Be someone people want to spend time with – cooperative, a team builder, a connector and a helping hand when something goes wrong. Be the person that champions other people, celebrates team wins (even when you're not involved), and offers to take someone for a drink when you can tell they're drowning in work. Being nice gets people far.

FIGURING OUT YOUR WORTH

I'm going to give you an insight into the way companies and clients work: they will almost always try their best not to pay you what you deserve. It took five jobs in six years for me to figure this out, but it happens everywhere – to everyone. The gender pay gap, racial bias and parental discrimination are just a few barriers that stop people getting what they're worth – all things that are sadly hard for us to control ourselves. But it doesn't mean we have to accept it. All the steps we've talked through so far should have got you in the mindset of being prepared to get your worth – and now I'll tell you how to action it.

NAVIGATING THE 'MONEY' CHAT

I want to tell you a story about a close friend of mine, Ella, who works in the finance industry. She'd joined an independent company – one that had more of a start-up culture than she expected. After putting her blood, sweat and tears into the role, it came to her annual review and they offered her a £700 increase for the year. That equated to less than £60 extra per month (and that's before tax!). Some might argue that at least it was an increase, but for someone who knew her contribution had directly improved the company's reputation and revenue, it was disappointing that the reward offered wasn't more representative of her input.

It was at this point that Ella had to decide whether to stay, knowing that this was the level of remuneration she was likely to get working at that specific company, or move on to get the money she deserved. So she did what *everyone should do* when going through a pay review, and searched around to see what the rest of the market might offer. Being highly skilled and talented in her field, she was invited to an interview at one of the industry's top firms, where she was offered £30k a year more than she was currently earning. Overnight, she went from being stuck with a £40k salary to knowing she could get £70k. FUCKING MENTAL. So what does that really tell us?

1   We very easily get stuck at companies that don't value us.

2   There are companies that will pay you more.

3   If you don't see what else is out there, you'll never understand your worth.

So what did Ella do next, I hear you ask. Well, she did what any clever money negotiator would do (more about this in the next chapter), and marched straight back to her current employer to share her new offer with them. She, of course, played it carefully and positioned herself as shocked that another company was able to offer her that much of an increased wage. She explained that it was too huge an offer not to consider, and felt it was only fair to be open and honest about it. And what did they do? They matched it. Through some 'miracle', despite only offering her £700 more a year before that, they managed to find an additional £30k to hold on to her and create a reason for her to stay.

Now, something tells me they always had those extra funds and they were purposely not paying her because they thought they could get away with it – because who in their right mind has ever asked an employer for a £30k increase and got it (without threatening to leave)? If it was that easy, we'd all be on £100k+ salaries and be wearing Gucci shoes.

So then what did she do? Well, she went back to the new company, explained the situation and they offered her £80k ... that's right, another £10k, meaning she had now officially DOUBLED HER SALARY. Pretty fucking impressive, right?! It was now even clearer what she needed to do ... one last negotiation. She went back to her current company to see what their final offer would be. They said they'd give her £100k (a £60k pay rise) – but she decided to walk. The truth was she'd never really had any intention of staying at a company that could undervalue her by that much. It's perhaps no surprise that this company was found to be in the top 30 per cent in terms of underpaying women when the most recent gender pay gap data came out.

Now, a big part of this story that I've not shared is that the job with the new company was a promotion and carried a lot more responsibility, longer hours and less time at home – so it's certainly not a fairy tale come to life. But she's now at a company that values her input so much that they reward it fairly and accurately.

Of course, the finance industry usually has higher salaries than those in other industries, so I wouldn't assume that every company will hand out a 100k offer – although nothing is impossible!

None of this negotiation would have happened had Ella not put herself out there. Had she not done her research, it could have been 10 years before she got that 40k pay rise and she'd have been unhappy in the process. Ella knew her abilities were worth more than she was receiving, and she used her knowledge in negotiations to get what she deserved.

HOW MUCH MONEY DO YOU REALLY NEED?

This is a question you probably rarely get asked or ask yourself. But when it comes to figuring out how much you value your abilities, it's something you have to consider to make sure you've got yourself covered. Later I'll dive into how you ask for it from others, but first I want you to ask yourself how much you actually want to earn.

Now before you throw a six-digit number at me, I mean think long and hard about the following:

1   How much money do you need to cover your overheads?

2   How much more money would you need to live a contented life?

3   What would you do with the additional money if you had it?

4   What are you willing to work for free for?

By breaking down your thinking around money, you'll start to be more specific about your reasons for wanting more – and more accurately quantify how much you need. I'll be the first to admit I've openly craved more money – but it's really thinking about what I'd use it for that gives me something concrete to strive towards.

It also helps you to figure out what you will and won't settle for. You might only need £1k a month to cover your outgoings, but you actually want to live a £2k-a-month lifestyle, and that means the amount you charge or the salary you accept needs to reflect that. Of course, do be a realist: if you're starting out in the industry but you want a £5k disposable income at the end of the month, you might have to be willing to sell a lot of shoes on Depop.

UNDERSTANDING YOUR INDUSTRY STANDARDS

The first thing I'd advise you to do once you've selected the role you're going after is to go online and research salaries for similar positions. How much are the big companies paying versus the small firms; what are the differences in levels, locations and responsibilities. You can do this on many sites and job boards such as Campaign Jobs, The Drum, Guardian Jobs and LinkedIn. If the salary isn't clearly advertised, you can also reach out to companies directly and ask them what the pay brackets are for specific roles.

Things to consider:

- A good tip is to compare industries too. If you're a graphic designer who wants a job at a fashion brand, it's worth seeing what rates are like in other industries. You might find that the catering and travel industries pay designers a higher rate, so keep an open mind about the sector you go for.

- When you're comparing salaries, remember to keep in mind what outgoings you might have if you were to take that job: would you spend more on travel, need more equipment or training – all things that could impact how much you actually take home.

- Make sure you review a company or client's standard base rate and expected hours.

- Check the company benefits, as often there are non-financial benefits that might actually mean more to you:

meditation Tuesdays, fresh fruit in the office, working-from-home days, and many more lovely things that money can't buy if your company isn't supporting them.

REQUEST THE JOB SPEC ABOVE YOURS

One of the best things you can do when starting a new job is to request the job spec of the role you're in for, but also the spec for the job above. I learned to do this in my career after expected promotions and pay rises didn't materialise – mainly down to the business financials. You'd be surprised how quickly companies will backtrack their commitments to you, and consequently leave you questioning your self-worth. So, to save your time and sanity, get the job spec of the level you're at and the level above that, and keep ticking off what you're doing as you're going along.

If your next role is to be a manager but you've not had the opportunity to manage people, raise it with your boss sooner rather than later. Stress that you're keen to move to the next level but that there are things that are limiting you – in this case, the fact that you aren't managing anyone. Let them take on that responsibility to find a solution and opportunity to demonstrate you're ready to move to the next level. By having the details of the more senior job, you can also set up regular catch-ups with your boss and request to take on more responsibilities, which shows them that you're ready to progress and also avoids a 'you've still got some areas you need to develop in' conversation. It's also a daily pre-made checklist that acts as a prompt to remind you of all the great things you're doing (no more questioning how qualified you are to do the job when it's a Monday and you're recovering from a heavy weekend).

If you're a freelancer and job specs aren't readily available, I would say you can use your workload, the types of projects and clients you're working with to see when you're improving. Asking for client feedback and testimonials is useful for you to understand what they enjoyed about working with you the most or what they would work with you on again. Another good resource is using mentors from within the industry as a guide of whether the level of work you're working on is now moving you from mid-weight to senior, something that we often struggle to notice ourselves (or feel comfortable awarding ourselves with!).

TALK TO YOUR PEERS INTERNALLY AND EXTERNALLY

Talking about salaries is up there with chats about the shapes of penises or wonky boobs – we avoid it even when it could help us the most. By speaking to colleagues about salaries and the remit of their role, you can gauge what the business might be willing to offer, understand where you're currently based and highlight the areas you might need to improve in to get paid at a similar level. By discussing it externally, you're able to get an objective opinion from people who might not be in the same industry but who probably understand your frustrations and can advise you on alternative ways to approach the money chat.

Sharing and comparing salary information with peers should not result in a negative conversation – see it as a wake-up call for you to take action. And if you're unsure of speaking to your direct peers, this is where having mentors will really come in useful!

REFLECTING ON ACHIEVEMENTS

In Chapter 2 we explored how to move away from commentating and towards storytelling, in order to put across a more compelling version of yourself. All that is great for raising awareness, but when it comes to communicating your self-worth you need to review your achievements and communicate them in a way that the person in control will *really* care about. From experience, even if you put in 110 per cent all year round, many companies might not reward you financially unless they can see how you've directly improved their business (and even then, they might not – be warned!). The same goes for freelancing or running your own business; people need to see the value exchange in order to invest.

So how do you make them see your value?! In short, be more Elle Woods.

Yes, I'm referencing one of the best/worst chick flicks from the early 2000s, *Legally Blonde,* but my point is that you need to prepare your case and understand how to attribute business value to your contributions. If you're fighting for more money, you have to demonstrate why you've earned it.

Let's look at five ways you can translate a personal achievement into business value you could be financially rewarded for:

- ## INTRODUCED A NEW CLIENT OR WORKED ON A SUCCESSFUL PITCH > INCREASED BUSINESS REVENUE

If you were involved in either recruiting a new client or putting together a successful pitch that has generated a new stream of income, leverage it. Make sure you write down exactly what your involvement was, how it helped the process, what you learned from it, and how you're now applying that level of expertise across the rest of your work. A company is there to make money, and if you can show your involvement in helping that happen, it's a no-brainer!

- ## CREATED AWARD-WINNING WORK > INCREASED BUSINESS AWARENESS

Let's say you designed something that received an industry award or generated awareness of the business through press. It's likely that your company will have grown its reputation based on your involvement. Document where the work has been shared and who has connected with the company since that project. Have you increased the reach geographically – or, even better, has it attracted new clients or employees? Always look at the different types of benefits your contribution brings, and don't be afraid to talk about all of them.

- ## IMPLEMENTED NEW PROCESSES > IMPROVED BUSINESS CULTURE OR SAVED MONEY

Very often you can go into a business and identify things that aren't right. Whether it's the software being used or company morale or spending on external suppliers, if you've helped change a company issue for the better, make sure you make a note of it. Remember to explain why those improvements made an impact to the business overall: changing software or company morale could lead to more efficiency from employees; changes in the way you deal with suppliers might save the company significant money, meaning there's more profit.

• ADDED NEW SKILLS > ENABLED NEW OPPORTUNITIES

Before *you* started working for your company or client, they might not have had the credibility to take on certain types of projects. If you're the only person in your department or you've been brought in specifically to solve a talent hole within the company, I imagine you're now enabling that company to have bigger conversations. Understand how integral you are to winning new clients, and how your skills are bringing in the business.

• BUILT LONG-TERM RELATIONSHIPS > GENERATED REPEAT BUSINESS

I've talked a lot about relationship-building in this book – because no matter what role you're in, if you're client-facing and delivering good-quality products on time, you're likely to be attracting repeat business. Any praise you receive externally, write it down. Any emails you receive telling you what a great job you did, save them. Any clients you've built a strong ongoing relationship with, make sure it's noticed. The more that people can see that your contribution is what drives these connections, the more you will be recognised and, hopefully, rewarded too.

These are my go-to tips for an interview, pay review or a pitch scenario to make sure that you're fully clued-in and up to date on your personal successes – to ensure you can ask for what you're truly worth. All this detail might seem laborious, but it will help you so much with quantifying exactly what you think you should earn. You've got to do the market trawl, the self-reflection reality checks – and you've got to stay on top of your own progress. Don't let waiting for your peers or managers be the barrier to not getting what you deserve.

NICOLE CRENTSIL

Cultural Producer & Co-Founder of Black Girl Festival

——

What's one of your best attributes and how did you figure it out?

'I think my best attribute is public speaking – I actually love it! I realised very quickly whilst studying product design at university that it wasn't all about creating the most beautiful product, but more about how I got to that final design, spoke about it and presented it back that was my forte. Towards the end of my final year, a lot of people would ask me to help them pitch and present their work, how to talk about it and how to have confidence. When I got my first job – and in my various other jobs – I set out to take all the skills and attributes that I loved about myself as a person and apply them to my work in any way I see fit. That actually made me feel like anything was possible and that I could walk into any job or any industry and just do it. I realised I could really pave my own way – and that all trickled down from me understanding, celebrating and being really forceful with that one attribute that I felt was really important to defining who I am.'

When was a time where you blagged your way through something and it paid off? How can people embrace the saying 'Blag now, worry later?'

'When I realised that loads of people blag their way through jobs, interviews and applications, I thought "What?! Okay, I'm definitely going to add a bit of colour and flavour to my application because if everyone else is doing it, why can't I?" I might know I'm not the usual candidate, but I know I can do it, so just give me the chance so I can prove to you – I'm the person you need. I feel like in the creative industry, a lot of people are blagging their way through it, because there are so many opportunities that aren't actually based on a specific skill.'

Do you battle with imposter syndrome? If so, what advice would you give to people trying to overcome it?

'The first time I really experienced imposter syndrome was when I created Unmasked Women. I hadn't connected with the other black women in the art world, so I had to teach myself everything – from the venue to the sponsors. I was honestly afraid to give myself the title of curator or producer because I feared someone would catch me out. I remember my mum saying to me, "You created it. Nobody else did this, you did this. You didn't have any institutional backing. You did this from scratch whilst working full-time, and you made it happen. So this is who you are, call yourself that." From that very moment I changed my bio on my social media platforms, I put it on my LinkedIn and added it to the bottom of my email signature. I got into the spirit and the practice of calling myself a producer. I became obsessed with celebrating the show I had created and the impact it had made. Because I was the one who did that.'

SIX

___

GETTING THE MONEY YOU WANT

S o, now you've done your market research, reflected on your contributions and processed what you're willing to accept (or walk away from), it's time to start making your voice heard.

Let's start with abolishing the saying 'Shall we address the elephant in the room?' It's quite literally one of my most hated phrases out there. Money shouldn't be the elephant in the room; if you worked for it, you've earned it. Whether you're pitching a project, bringing up your freelance day rate or discussing a pay rise, you've most likely put in a level of effort that deserves to be rewarded. But by mentioning that very phrase, you yourself *create* the 'elephant' in the room.

Much like self-promotion, us Brits are particularly bad at talking about money (unless we're complaining about not having it), but we need to learn to normalise the conversation. Periods and female masturbation weren't an 'acceptable' thing to talk about not that long ago, and yet somehow the world now knows periods aren't blue and girls do in fact like to orgasm. When we're overly reserved about the conversation, we help position it as a taboo topic and often settle for less, because we haven't taken the initiative to be more inquisitive. It's time to start opening up, embracing the topic and making sure we all get what we deserve.

I often break down the simplicity of financial reflection as: YOU ARE IN YOUR FINANCIAL SITUATION BECAUSE OF YOU. AND ONLY YOU CAN CHANGE IT.

Now, before you get out your long list of people or situations that you hold accountable for your financial state, listen to me when I say that the two things you *do* control are:

1   YOUR SOURCE(S) OF INCOME

2   HOW YOU SPEND IT

Don't worry, I'm definitely not going to lecture you about how to spend your money (bearing in mind I've spent significant time on MoneySavingExpert.com and have considered modelling for life-drawing classes when skint at the end of the month) – this is just a dose of reality that people rarely give us. Your job might not always give you the money you need or want, so it's up to you to either find an alternative cash flow or change the way you currently approach your finances.

Mathieu Ajan, the founder of Bounce Cinema, explained it very simply to me when we first met: 'Money is everywhere; if you want it you can get it. You might have to sacrifice things or even put in an initial investment to start off, but you can find money anywhere.' And he couldn't be more right. Our world revolves around money, and whether it's selling things on eBay, taking on a part-time job or taking on more responsibilities to earn a higher salary, we can all make more money – but we have to put in the effort to get it and have the confidence to ask for it.

A quote from Jen Sincero's book *You Are a Badass at Making Money* supports this attitude: 'Where there's a will there's a way; we just prefer to pretend there isn't a way so we don't have to take responsibility and do the uncomfortable stuff required to grow.' People love to complain about money as a way to deflect responsibility – but when you take a step back, you choose to work in the job you have and the hours you give. By staying in the situation you're in, you're choosing to have the same amount of money in your bank account every month. You're choosing to have a gym membership, eat out for dinner and have both a Netflix and a Prime account even though you barely use both. To take control of your financial destiny, let's explore when the optimum times are to speak up about getting more money.

STRIKE WHEN THE IRON IS HOT

When you're navigating your way through your career, it's very easy to get tunnel vision and only focus on your own trajectory. Don't get me wrong, I'll always encourage you to focus on your road to success, but try not to let your solo mission obscure the external factors that could affect whether you're getting the money you deserve.

What I mean by 'external factors' is that there are so many things a company has to consider when it comes to spreading the love financially, and they're not always as black and white as you think. I say this from experience because I've been an employee who has asked for more money at the wrong time, not received it, and then stewed about it for the next six months. (Which, by the way, isn't healthy for your mental state, nor does it make you enjoyable to be around.) So before you go all 'Leo DiCaprio in *The Wolf of Wall Street*' in your next review or client meeting because they don't give you what you want, I'd highly advise you to do due diligence on a company's past, present and future state.

PAST

A lot of the issues involved in a business not remunerating their staff appropriately won't be new. So before you get yourself into an awkward situation, it's always good to give the company a financial audit.

Don't worry, you don't need to be good at maths. All you need to do is find out how the company is viewed in the industry. Are they notorious for underpaying? Do they only recruit people with a certain level of experience or credibility? How long have they been running? Has it been a successful journey, or have finances caused issues in the past? Do they replace people quickly and easily or do they have long-standing members of staff?

Finding out the answers to these questions ahead of beginning the relationship will help you to decide whether it's worth partnering with the company, and prepare you for how you approach your money plans with them. If you ask around and you find out that a company doesn't give out regular pay increases, then you know you need to negotiate a higher rate upfront. The more research you do in advance, the less likely you are to be disappointed halfway down the line. Read articles online, ask old employees, check Glassdoor reviews – do your social stalking and try to understand more about their values, approach and style of business.

PRESENT

It's usually not hard to detect when a business is doing well financially. Media coverage, new cash injections and new business or recruitment advertisements are all indicators that finances are healthy. As we discussed in the previous chapter, if you can associate your own input with the business success, it's going to be much easier to justify a higher increase in pay. And if you're a freelancer observing a potential client's recent success, get yourself on their radar and strike while the iron is hot. Just like payday and the generous amounts of shots from strangers that get passed around, make the most of the positive wave and ride it for as long as you can. If a company's not doing well but you feel you still deserve to be rewarded as an employee or can offer your freelance services, pitch with passion and make yourself heard but be prepared to have to manage your emotions in the room if you don't get what you're looking for.

FUTURE

Understanding what's in the pipeline for a business is probably the most important factor in negotiating more money. I spent roughly six weeks feeling frustrated in a previous job when I didn't get the pay increase I requested, and it was only in a follow-up review that they explained the decision was based on whether the company won the pitches we had in the pipeline. As soon as we did, they gave me the money I asked for.

It's really important not only to focus on the now, but to also make sure you have an understanding of where the business is – or isn't – going financially. (And if you're a boss managing this process, just let your staff know that's what's going on rather than letting them convince themselves they're not good enough!) Just because a company has seen an influx of cash or project work doesn't mean it will be retained. Increased overheads and changes in company spending might mean the pot available to reward staff is still low, so dig deeper and enquire about the business's growth plans in order to choose the optimum time to ask for more. Set up regular meetings with your bosses and ask them straight out, 'How's the next six to twelve months looking for new business?' Or sit down with the finance team and see if they're open to explaining the company's financial status. It shows that you're thinking long term and are taking a commercial interest in the company.

HOW TO TALK ABOUT MONEY

PITCH WITH PASSION

We've all seen those episodes of *Dragons' Den* where everything seems to be going swimmingly until the conversation about numbers starts, and it's not long until Duncan Bannatyne's cutting Scottish accent interrupts them and ends their pitch with an 'I'm out'. Every time I see it happen, all I can think is, *If only they'd prepared that bit more, known their company inside out and spoken with confidence, they wouldn't be waving goodbye to their spray-on pants concept.*

The key to pitching with confidence is preparation. The more you put into preparing for conversations about future developments – be it relationships, money or promotions – the better they'll go. So, once you've done your homework on the past, present and future of the company, you can think about how to use that information strategically to get your desired outcome.

Need help with presenting? Well, if you don't already know Alexandria Ocasio-Cortez, then get to know her. Her Twitter account is an amazing resource for public speaking inspiration, and after months of analysing why she's so bloody good, I've come to the conclusion that she not only really understands and believes her arguments, she can articulate them in a captivating and convincing way. Follow her combination of clarity, conviction and presence (CCP) and I have no doubt you'll put a great case forward.

PRACTICE MAKES PERFECT

Once you've prepped that narrative, it's time to start practising it. As someone who has done her fair share of interviews, networking and asking for pay rises, I can honestly say that the more you practise the conversation in advance, the better the outcome will be. I've always been lucky to have my parents and sister to practise with, and I can rely on them to throw in some squeamish quick-fire 'just in case they ask' questions that, although I hate them at the time, do actually come in handy. But if they weren't around, I'd practise alone (in a private space where speaking to myself was socially acceptable), to get myself familiar with what I'm saying and why I'm saying it. Hopefully, after reading this book you'll be documenting your achievements more regularly, ticking off your job spec capabilities and recognising how you're adding business value, so when it comes to asking for more money, it's more about perfecting the pitch than it is about believing in yourself in the first place.

> *Top tip: If you're worried you're going to forget anything, just take all your talking points in on your laptop or a notepad and refer back to them throughout the conversation. It doesn't make you look any less confident, and it makes sure you don't forget anything if for any reason you find yourself getting flustered!*

BE BOLD WITH SUGGESTIONS

Badass of the British creative industry Cindy Gallop is famous for encouraging women to embrace and demand their self-worth – so much so that she even created chatbot to help women asking for a raise. She says, 'You should ask for the highest number you can utter without actually bursting out laughing.' It's common for companies to attempt to negotiate you down anyway, so it's usually best to aim high the first time round.

What she says is absolutely right, because if you yourself don't believe the number you're asking for, then the decision makers in control definitely won't. When a global brand contacted me to give a workshop for their internal teams, I knew it was time to up my speaker fee but I wasn't sure how high I could go – so I spoke to my friend, life coach Adam Parker, who suggested I choose a number and then double it. Although it made sense and was in line with Cindy's advice, like many people do, I questioned whether I had the balls to do it. But when I did, I didn't get laughed out of the room. This was a huge victory – not just because they didn't blink an eyelid at the cost, but because I had set a new value for my offering. I could now confidently say this number again, knowing that it had been accepted once before. And as I further grow my skills and reputation I continue to increase my rate – it's about having the courage to ask for what you know you deserve.

LEAVE YOUR EMOTIONS AT THE DOOR

Much easier said than done, granted. But it's important for you to remain as gracious as possible and display objectivity. Body language is key: sit in a relaxed manner, maintain eye contact and nod your head regularly (even if what you really want to do is throw a brick at the other person's head). My sister has always said that you can't control anyone else's actions but you can control your own emotions. Remember this when you feel rage, despair or even floods of tears building up: you control your financial situation, and this is just one resource for you. There are always other ways.

A big tip is to be mindful of rambling and over-justifying your requests. This is another reason why preparation is key. Let them respond before you start up an endless 'this is why I'm great' chant or a 'please pay me this, I promise I'm worth it' plea.

USE THE RIGHT WORDS

On a recent panel I moderated on making money, panellist Zoe Bayliss Wong, Finance Director at Depop, advised that you should avoid using the word 'deserve' in money meetings. You can totally feel like you deserve that fee in your head, but try to use more fact-driven and objective vocab to emphasise why. Keep the emotion out of it!

From my own personal experience of watching different types of money negotiations, I always encourage people to avoid phrases like:

* Yes, of course I can <u>cut my fee</u>!
* <u>I've</u> done so much for <u>you</u>.
* Why are they getting paid <u>more than me</u>?

And instead use:

* Based on my <u>research</u> ...
* The <u>market value</u> for this role ...
* <u>Other clients</u> I work with ...
* This would be a <u>great opportunity</u> ...

By taking out the personal language, you're able to give a more grounded and mature pitch to communicate why you deserve what you're asking for. Have your notes close to hand and refer to them if you feel things are getting too subjective; remember: you've earned it, so that's why you're asking for it.

UNDERSTAND WHO YOU'RE SPEAKING TO AND WHAT MAKES THEM TICK

Not everyone is going to have the same empathy towards your financial frustrations as your roommates in your damp flat do, so think about the person making the decision and what they care most about. How can you use that to your advantage and draw them in to see eye to eye?

If they've got a family of their own, for example, they might be more likely to understand if you want to change your hours to be more flexible. It can also be helpful to understand their journey through the business, what they are looking for most in employees and how you've helped to improve their specific agenda. It's much easier to get the results you want when you find a common ground and demonstrate how you're working towards the same positive results.

RESPONDING TO BAD NEWS

If you're yet to have to hear the news that your request for a certain figure hasn't been granted, lucky you. It's a killer whatever stage you're at in your career, but remember to keep your language objective and your physical gestures calm, and try to understand why the decision has been made.

It's important be constructive and ask for more information. So, if you hear 'We'd like to offer you 10p extra', respond with:

* Is there any flexibility in the amount?
* How have you arrived at this figure?
* I am looking for a figure between (£30–40k).

If they tell you 'We have no budget', respond with:

* What is the reason for this outcome?
* When will it be reviewed?

* Can we put a payment plan in place?
* Is there any other way my work could be rewarded?

Pushing them to give you answers will help provide further clarity and help you to digest the situation. You might instinctively want to just squirm out of the room and avoid the conversation, but make sure you have explored and documented their reasoning so you have something to refer back to. As humans, we like to dwell on the negatives, but if you have the reasons given to you, you can focus on working on a new approach to get what you want.

I DON'T GET PAID TO AT 10 DOWNING STRE MY TIME WILL EVENT

SHANICE MEARS, THE ELEPHANT ROOM & FOUNDER OF GIRLS LET'S TALK

T ON THE BOARD
T BUT I KNOW THAT
ALLY BE PAID FOR.

THE FOLLOW-UP

I recently got the advice to always CYA (Cover Your Arse) when it comes to pay and performance reviews. Just like with any meeting, you can easily get swept up in the moment, agree lots of great things and then never see results or a follow-up. Appoint yourself the role of following up to avoid disappointment or delays. Write up everything you discussed, share it with the purse-strings holder, and ask them to review it and to input any further comments or things you may have missed. Depending on the outcome of the conversation, you might need to take one or more of the following steps ...

FIND A SONG

There are two songs you need in your life: a fuck-you song and a celebration song. If you don't get the answer you want, select a fuck-you song that you can listen to on repeat until the anger is no longer in your system and you've moved on from wanting to sucker-punch your boss. My personal favourite was singing Big Sean's 'I don't give a fuck' repeatedly for weeks (ironically, because I clearly did give a fuck).

If, however, everything goes according to plan, make sure you've got something upbeat and motivational to blare out in celebration. Both your fuck-you song and your celebration song are a great form of release – and, speaking from experience, they genuinely helped me through every outcome.

BE CLEAR ABOUT WHAT'S INCLUDED

When confirming salary and rates, make sure that there is full transparency about what is and isn't included in your fee. I've spent years creating client budgets that have a very clear 'Exclusions' list that highlights what isn't included so no one gets screwed over. Whether it's hours, expectations or responsibilities, make sure that when you discuss a figure, both parties are clear on what's required. You don't want to sign your life away to an unattainable workload or lifestyle for the sake of a couple of extra quid. If you're a freelancer, it's always worth drafting up a scope of work document along with your quote and making sure they're signed by key stakeholders before you begin a project.

SET UP REGULAR CATCH-UPS

If you're not happy with your salary but you've decided not to leave the company, then make sure you set up follow-ups to ensure you're on the right path to getting your rewards. Don't give your boss an excuse to hide behind – be prepared, be punctual, and stay on top of your expectations and development.

I'd also set yourself a deadline for a change to be made. This is for your sanity, so you don't blink and realise three years have gone and promises were never fulfilled. Try drawing up a timeline for your goals with your manager – if you're subjected to a continuous string of let-downs, then you'll know it's the right time to part ways.

ASSESS YOUR LONG-TERM GAIN

So you didn't get the job title or the pay rise you wanted, but is that enough to make you throw it all away? Think about the bigger picture and any benefits you gain from being at your company that aren't financial – do they make up for not getting as much money? Is working with them going to grow your skills, build your reputation, or open doors you might not be able to access without them?

Whatever you do, make sure you're pushing for regular business updates and have an understanding of the business's future so you can make a clear decision. It's worth giving yourself at least a month to reflect on what the real positives are about working for your company – and more importantly, to figure out whether you've still got the appetite to do it.

START PREPPING FOR YOUR PLAN B

If plan A fails, it's time to start actioning your backup plan, to help make the time you have left at the company as bearable as possible. If you wanted to progress to manager level but the company said you don't have the experience, ask to be sent on a training course and let them pay for your development (whether you plan to stay or not). Or, if being overworked for your pay bracket is what's bothering you, start going home on time and build a team around you to help lighten your load while you plan your exit strategy. There's no point sitting there being unhappy – get the most out of the company, and get yourself in the best shape to move on.

RETAINING YOUR CONFIDENCE

There's no denying that your confidence can and will most likely be knocked if you don't get your desired outcome; it's a killer, and in many cases it's unavoidable. Top tips to make sure you don't let a bad review get the best of you:

1 Go through your achievements clearly with your manager, and make sure you understand what you're missing.

2 Speak to someone externally about the situation: tap up a mentor or even a friend, and talk them through how you're feeling.

3 Surround yourself with people who *do* see your positive qualities – be it in your professional or personal life. It'll ensure you experience the feeling of recognition in some parts of your life, at least.

4 Interview for other jobs to gain experience and feedback on where you're positioned outside of your company.

5 Review your personal and professional goals. Can you readjust the time you invest and refocus how your energy is being spent?

6 Spend time working on projects or hobbies that you *do* feel confident in, to build yourself up again.

7 Make a list of inspirational podcasts about people who overcame failure and setbacks. *How to Fail, Lecture in Progress* and *How I Built This* are a few I'd recommend.

8 Find a support space where you can seek out guidance. The Other Box platform is a great resource for advice, stories, courses, events and people to collaborate with.

9 Journal your emotions and write down the areas you feel you've been affected by (see Chapter 1). This is a good way to figure out whether it's a temporary low mood or if there are specific triggers.

10   Speak to people – friends and family, mentors and colleagues – and seek out support. You don't have to get through this alone.

Every year, month, week and day that you negotiate money, you will discover the best way to sell your skills. There's definitely no one-size-fits-all approach, and you will almost always have to adapt to fit the needs of the person paying you. But as you grow and become more comfortable with negotiations, do remember to be open to speaking about money, seek out support, listen to books and podcasts – anything to help you mix up your tactics. You deserve the money you ask for, you just need to package up your request in a way that fully demonstrates your value.

ZOE BAYLISS WONG

Finance Director at Depop

———

What's one of your best attributes and how did you figure it out?

'For me it's emotional intelligence. I worked it out because it was one of those things that I used to comment on in meetings and people would ask, "How did you realise that's how that person was feeling or thinking?" It felt obvious to me, but I think realising what people find to be really hard and what you find to be really easy is probably the best way to work on what you know. You can't really get anywhere without a team and taking people with you. One of the most important things is to really understand what other people might be worried about versus what you're worried about. It's not just thinking about what your goals are, but what everyone else's goals are too. It's all about teamwork.'

When was a time where you blagged your way through something and it paid off? How can people embrace the saying 'Blag now, worry later?'

'I went to the Forbes Under 30 annual conference that they do every year and I remember walking into it and thinking, "Oh my God, most people here have done something amazing, they're either CEOs from a really famous brand or they're saving lives, and I'm just this accountant that works at a marketplace." I had to just go in and say to myself, "Pretend you're one of these people and just go in with that amount of confidence." And I did, and I ended up speaking to so many great people, who were super-well-connected, but if I knew what they had done before I probably wouldn't have spoken to them. But giving yourself that kind of mental boost and blagging internally is really great for those situations.'

Getting the money you deserve can be tricky. What's the best money advice you could give to get what you're worth?

'As a manager and someone who approves pay rises, I think one of the most important things that you can do is set aside a time to talk about it. It's not just about tacking it on as the last point in your one-to-one with your manager; it's actually setting aside a separate conversation where you don't accidentally blindside your manager, so that they can be best-prepared and maybe be able to give you a positive answer straight away because they knew that that's what you're talking about in the first place. Then also continue to follow up because silence doesn't necessarily mean it's a no. Silence sometimes can mean that it's been forgotten or it's waiting on someone else in management to chase someone.'

———————————

SEVEN

CALM THE
F*CK DOWN

L ife is an emotional rollercoaster; you've just got to know how to ride it. (Yes, I am paraphrasing Ronan Keating, but for good reason ...)

You know that stupid interview question where they ask you to list something negative about yourself and you know you can only really answer with a positive otherwise you're literally damaging your rep before you've even started?! Well, mine is usually that I'm too emotional.

Not in the sense that I'm shedding tears every day, more that I'm someone who gets emotionally invested in my work and sometimes struggles to step away from it. Of course, to an employer I might sound a little clingy, but it's one of those negatives that demonstrates my passion for the job. Plus, for me, being emotional in your career isn't a bad thing, and nor should it be in your personal life either. Whether it's being happy, angry, calm or diplomatic, emotions showcase your personality and help you to understand what you care about in life. When you have an awareness of your own emotional triggers and those of others around you, you will have more control over situations and can often create more positive outcomes.

This is what we call 'emotional intelligence', or EI. Managing your own emotions, listening to others so they feel heard, showing empathy, learning from your mistakes and being open to receiving feedback are all examples of emotional intelligence. It's one of those highly respected skills that so many people haven't quite cracked, but it will completely change your career and how well you're perceived.

In order to nail self-promotion in a way that doesn't make people want to punch you in the face for having your head up your own arse, you've got to understand the power that emotional intelligence will play. It's the difference between coming across as confident instead arrogant, intelligent instead of a know-it-all, decisive instead of dominating. The message of 'F*ck Being Humble' can only be put into practice if you understand the foundations of emotional intelligence and how crucial it is to learn from your own emotions and those of others.

I've spent my entire career trying to understand people and their behaviours. My role inherently means I'm the middleman every single day, and I'm often absorbing emotions externally (from my clients) and internally (from colleagues) – and yes, it really is as intense as it sounds. But I learned quite early on that the sooner you understand what makes different people tick or explode, the sooner you can manage your relationships with them and get the outcome you want. Don't get me wrong, it's not an easy journey and you might spend months or even years trying to crack that one person who does your head in, but the more time you invest in learning about their individual character traits, the less time you'll waste getting upset or feeling let down.

There are far too many emotions to cover all in one chapter, but here are some of the most career-focused emotions you'll no doubt have to deal with, both in yourself and others around you – and how to manage them as well as you possibly can.

ADAPTABILITY IN YOURSELF

Adaptability is all about being open to change. As I've grown up, I've noticed that there are two types of change: change you can control and change that is out of your control. The first kind includes things like choosing a better broadband service to get faster internet, or choosing the full-fat Coke over Diet Coke to nurse your hangover, or days out in the countryside because you need a change from the big city life. It's choosing a solution that suits what you need – there and then – for the better. This is the type of change we like and we're comfortable with in our lives.

The change we despise is when it's out of our control. It's when decisions are made for us and we don't have a say in the matter. When people say they're terrible with change, it's usually not all change – they're talking about the type that makes you feel like you've had the wool pulled over your eyes and you're in a straitjacket of limitations. Here are some examples:

1   When your train is delayed, meaning you're going to be late.

2   When your phone battery runs out and you don't know where you're going.

3   When you lose a team member and you had no control over it.

4   When your date cancels last minute and you've spent two hours getting ready.

5   When you get toothpaste down your outfit as you're walking out the door.

Now, you may well have had an irrational meltdown for any or all of these reasons (I know I have), but even though you didn't plan for these changes, you will have found a solution. Maybe not one you would have chosen in an ideal world, but you found one. Remember this, because it is this type of change that we have to get better at dealing with – because we live in a world where unexpected changes happen every minute of the day, and sitting around sulking will get you nowhere. And we all know that always having the same approach to problem-solving makes things stagnant. You end up limiting yourself and your capabilities in a negative way; you become a specialist in your own approach but not good at any other.

A big thing we have to remember is that, in this era of human versus tech that is fast approaching, it's our ability to react and adapt that outperforms machine thinking. Machines aren't always programmed to find a new solution – but we are.

Here's my top advice on how to be better at adapting ...

HAVE AN OPEN MIND

Even if in your head you are 99 per cent convinced that your way of doing things is the best possible way, it's important to be challenged. You don't have to necessarily action other suggestions immediately, but at least be open to listening to how you could alter your approach. We all know that horrible feeling of wanting to give feedback but knowing that person will never change. So don't be that inflexible person. Make yourself known as someone who is open to taking advice and feedback – and don't take it personally when it's given to you.

DON'T HOLD A GRUDGE

I think my boyfriend can vouch for the fact that, although I do a lot of problem-solving in my everyday life, sometimes I struggle with unforeseen dramas that fly our way. A particular story that sticks out was our first night in Bangkok together, when we got conned into paying £100 for a ping-pong show. It was irritating and embarrassing that we'd been scammed by the most touristy thing after a mere four hours of being in the city. And while I spent 30 minutes cursing Tom for being naive enough to be led in, I knew in my head I just needed to be annoyed for an hour and then I'd be fine. We did a lap round the block and noticed we'd actually been scammed by an extremely low-quality bar, then we laughed, found a nightclub and danced the bad mood away. You might not be attending ping pong shows with colleagues or career connections, but there may well be times when someone steps on your toes or even claims your ideas as their own (intentionally or not).

Be the person that gets over things quickly and doesn't ruin the vibe, even if you're bottling it up so you can explode when you get home.

BREAK AWAY FROM HABITS

What you fear most about a change you can't control might be not knowing how it will leave you feeling. Instead, you focus on consistency, structure, patterns and making similar choices. In doing this, you become a creature of habit – and new things thrown at you will continue to scare you. But as we spoke about in the introduction, you weren't born into this world an expert in anything – you tried things until you found what you liked.

Keep trying new things, meeting new people, experimenting with new techniques and reading new books, and watch as you continue to find new approaches.

DON'T REJECT CHANGE JUST BECAUSE IT DIDN'T WORK OUT WELL THE FIRST TIME

You didn't stop going to McDonald's the first time you threw it up after a boozy night, so remember not to fall straight back into the same patterns if you don't see immediate improvements. Elizabeth Day's podcast *How To Fail* celebrates how failing can help to shape people – and the vast majority of the people she interviews are a high-flying success. We'll get on to why failures make you funny shortly, but ultimately you can always learn from a failure – you've just got to be open to finding different ways to embrace change.

MAKE PEOPLE AWARE YOU'RE WILLING TO ADAPT

People have preconceived ideas of what you can and can't manage, but unless you let people know you can adapt and you're willing to be flexible, they could pigeonhole you as only being suitable for certain things. Being an adaptable employee or client is a desirable quality because it demonstrates your ability to thrive in different situations. Don't let what people think they know about you dictate how you're seen for future opportunities.

ADAPTABILITY IN OTHERS

In almost all jobs, there's always that one person who has been there for 15 years. They're usually grumpy, stuck in their ways and not particularly friendly to new people – and do you know what they are? Adaptability-phobes. Everyone around them makes excuses for their behaviour or their lack of integration, and you end up tiptoeing around them because it's not the done thing to challenge them, and people just say things like, 'Don't take it personally, you know Dave, that's just what he's like.' I don't know about you, but I find that excuse the most infuriating thing to hear, because we all know that if I went round telling everyone to piss off every two minutes, people would be a little less understanding of 'what I'm like'.

These people don't like to adapt because they're not forced to. Whether it's new ways of working, welcoming new types of people or exploring different communication techniques, they're the first to reject an idea and make it clear they're not getting involved. I wish I could tell you that you won't find this in every place you work, but whether it's a colleague, boss or client, you will always face adaptability-phobes.

So how the hell do you manage other people's resistance and inability to change? Much like negotiations, or building up team morale, you need to have a strategy – and it looks like this:

- ## LISTEN FIRST

Most people who resist new things or challenge new approaches have usually had a failed experience that taints their enthusiasm, so the first thing you should do is try to figure out what's rubbed them up the wrong way. By doing this, you can not only empathise with them and show that you acknowledge their concerns, you can work their issue into your strategy and show how your solution will help them.

- ## PUT THE WORDS IN THEIR MOUTH

Once you've got to the root of their resistance and you think you've found a way to manage it, it's time to tell them the plan. But rather than going in for all the glory, this is where you allude to your solution without giving it away – instead involving them in the thinking process and making it a collaborative approach. Dialogue like 'Wouldn't it be great if we could find a solution for ...' or 'the current solution isn't working – how do you think we could make it work?' lets them feel like they're originating the idea (even though you are framing the questions in the direction of your solution).

Remember, people fear change when it's out of their control, so let them think they had a part in fixing it to get them on board.

- ## TRIAL IT

The reason we love a trial period for a gym, mattress or car is that we need to feel like we really want it before we can commit to spending our time and money on it. The same goes for instilling change and making people feel comfortable about it – so where possible, always try to introduce the change as a trial or pilot scheme. By using these terms, you're saying it's not permanent until you see a positive impact – and it lets others feel more open to trying it out. A pilot or trial makes sense for you too, because you don't have to be wedded to the idea if it doesn't work out. Treat it like a mini case study, and once you get good results, you'll have more ammunition to encourage change. People want to see proof – so show them new ways of thinking work, so they have little reason to resist.

• FIND ADAPTABILITY ADVOCATES

Much like having Pharrell front a sustainability campaign helps to win over the masses, sometimes you need to find allies who will champion and embrace adaptability in order to encourage change. Just like in those films where the preppy guy picks the geeky girl and then all the popular kids welcome her with open arms, how can people who have influence help you to drive the change you're look-ing for and bring the tribe with them? Who are the micro-influencers that you can lean on to make your mission cool? No one wants to feel left out, even if they are stubborn – so maybe the message has to come from other people to lure in those resisters.

• BE OPEN-MINDED, BUT DON'T LOSE YOURSELF

Of course, there are going to be times where you have to work harder or spend more time finding solutions to approach situations with adaptability phobes, but remember that all you can really control are your own actions. Some people may never change; so it's about knowing that you kept it professional, you adapted your own processes and you offered up solutions that could work (if they weren't willing to engage). Losing sleep over it isn't going to help anyone, especially you, so figure out whether their stubbornness is something you can change or whether you need to leave it behind as their issue to solve.

ANGER IN YOURSELF

Anger can take many forms – rage, frustration or even the feeling that anyone who crosses your path you'll rip to shreds – and it's something we all come across and feel. It can be internalised to the point where your head is going to blow off because you've gone over the situation so many times, played out every possible situation and still feel no sense of relief. Or it can be externalised, turning into a one-way, slightly embarrassing argument with the printer which later turns into an office meme doing the rounds on the all-staff email thread. However you choose to let off steam is up to you, but being careful about the *when* and *where* is the key to controlling your emotion in an intelligent way. Anger is a trait that can drive people away and create a negative stigma around your persona; we've spent 90 per cent of this book focusing on how you bring your best attributes to the surface, so don't let your temper be the thing that changes people's opinion of you.

First things first, if you need to leave the situation to simmer down (and can do so without causing a scene), do that straight away. Graciousness in difficult situations is way more respected than verbally undressing someone with petty comebacks or threatening to take the company to court. Go for a walk, have a cigarette if you're a smoker, call the first name in your phone book – or, my personal favourite, eat the emotion away. Once you've done a couple (or 10) laps of the block, come back and write everything you're feeling down. That common feeling of eruption usually occurs because you've bottled your feelings up, but the minute you write it down, you're one step closer to letting it go. It also gives you the opportunity to reflect on what you are most angry about, who said what, and what you want to do to change the situation. You now have it documented, so you can come back to this if the emotion or problem arises again.

Now, not all situations will allow you to do a quick 'lose your shit' walk; in those instances, you need to remember that your reaction will dictate the result of the issue at hand. In almost all cases, not responding outwardly and publicly is going to be the best solution, mainly because you need to allow yourself time to gather your thoughts and react rationally. Responding with an immediate emotion won't allow you the time to consider all the angles or possible resolutions. Of course, if you're still feeling an uncontrollable rage 48 hours later, you know you need to revisit the issue, but at least this way you will have given yourself time to provide a considered solution.

One of the most effective things I do is to confide in people I can trust – both related and unrelated to the situation. Just like all big decisions in life, comparing and contrasting different people's opinions helps to give you a more well-rounded perspective, and may even teach you to avoid this trigger again. Whether it's a mentor or a partner, it's important you offload onto people you can trust to have your best interests at heart, both professionally and emotionally. But don't let your venting turn into a bitchfest, and try to remain professional when discussing the situation. Bad-mouthing has helped no one ever.

Once you've talked it through with the right people, you need to seek the right help. I say 'right' help because one size doesn't fit all; it's about getting to the root of the particular issue, the people involved, the variables that can change and those that can't. Your anger doesn't need to be permanent if you discuss it with the right people. Internally, there are CEOs, HR, directors and office managers who should be able to deal with the situation; and externally, you can turn to mentors, life coaches, therapists or even your best mate on the phone. When you reach out to these people, try to make sure you have solutions to offer up, think about the multiple end outcomes you'd like to see; this will show that it's not a reactive moan but a problem you want to address.

Most importantly, do not neglect anger. Tackle it head on and get to the root of the issue. By ignoring the symptoms, you can – and most likely will – become bitter towards the trigger, whether it be a person or a situation. It might continue to be a sore spot for the rest of your life, and you'll risk reacting more sensitively to it later on, due to the culmination of years of carrying the anger around. Yes, we are allowed to be angry, but it's what you do with that anger that will help to remove it from your life.

ANGER IN OTHERS

For the first 11 months of my career, I was an emotional punchbag for my unhinged boss, who would offload his inexplicable anger on me and the little team we had, day in, day out. My relationship with him was an odd one. I always got the feeling he looked at me like his protégé, but I often found him competing with me, putting me down, and emotionally abusing me and my confidence. One memory that truly sticks out was him speeding through country lanes on the way to a pitch for which I'd apparently not 'properly' bound the document (this will make sense to anyone born before 2000). Because of that and the fact he felt completely out of his depth, he did what can only be described as 'losing his shit'. While weaving in and out of traffic at 100 miles per hour – one evil eye on the road and the other piercing my left cheek – he reeled off every swear word under the sun, repeatedly screeching that I and the team were a waste of time and didn't deserve to breathe the same air as him.

This was all made worse by the fact that we were in his crap tiny sports car, where the feeling of claustrophobia overwhelmed me and I felt like I was actually running out of air. I'd been working at the company for six months by that point, so his behaviour wasn't new – in fact, his anger and lack of control were daily occurrences. One thing he liked about me, however, was that I'd always tell him the truth; I'd be straight up and not pussyfoot around him and his antics. But at that specific moment, in which I was truly scared for my safety, I used my best defence mechanism: silence. I took in everything he said and stayed quiet, but my jaw was clenched so tightly even he could see the reshaping of my face. I knew deep down he wanted me to shout back – I could see it in his eyes, he was trying to evoke the reaction that all bullies look for. But calling on all the self-restraint I had to hand, I didn't get sucked in. I stayed calm and waited for him to get every last bit of hot air out, then got out of the car and did the pitch.

As someone who doesn't shy away from confrontation, even against someone who looked like a possessed version of Meatloaf, I was proud of myself for taking the high road (excuse the pun). After the pitch, he finally clocked my intentional silence and simmered down enough for me to explain why his behaviour was completely unacceptable. It didn't change him, but at least I kept my dignity, and didn't let myself stoop to his level.

I tell that story because being the victim of someone else's anger resulted in weekly Sunday-evening tears, as the fear of the weekend ending and the thought of going back to work descended. And even though I championed my thick skin around the office, I knew inside I was on the edge of crumbling – and even questioning whether I was ever going to be good at my job. I'd started to worry that the minor mistakes he would go mad about were really much bigger problems I wasn't taking seriously enough.

The only upside to the experience is that no one will ever compare to how bad it was with him. To get me through my time working at that company I did the following things, and if you're in a similar situation I would recommend you try them too:

1   INVESTIGATE TRIGGERS

There could be a number of different things provoking someone's anger and it might not actually be your fault.

Make it your mission to figure out what the real problems are. Is it their workload, a lack of support or even personal issues? Try to take them away from the office, as they're more likely to open up in a casual setting. You might not uncover the issue the first time but keep chipping away, watching their behaviour in different situations and seeing if there are peak times when the anger occurs. Once you can identify the patterns or triggers, you can plan ways to stop them from happening or prepare yourself for the inevitable.

2   TRY A MIXTURE OF TACTICS

Mix up how you react to the person's anger and see what the outcome is. My sister actually bought me a book on how to deal with difficult bosses one year, and I've never let it out of my sight. Whether it's repeating back what they've said so they can hear how OTT they're being, or deferring to a third party to see how they would manage it. See what calms them down or riles them up; it may change from day to day, but there's no harm in trying everything – you'll know from the response what's working well!

3   LOG EVERYTHING IN A LITTLE BLACK BOOK

I know I've banged on about it throughout this whole book, but documenting your career is honestly your saviour when you have to manage the anger of others. Write down what happened, who else was involved, your response and how it made you feel. This works as a constant reminder that it's not all in your head, and if you find yourself writing about incidents on more than 20 occasions, then it's time to move on. If things really go down the drain, you also have documentation if you need to escalate it.

4   TALK TO ALLIES

It's very easy to internalise your feelings so much that you end up blaming yourself for the actions of others, but the one thing that can get you through a tough time is the support of the people around you. Because sometimes you need to go on a rant at lunch or cry in the toilets, and knowing you've got someone to support you through it or cover for you helps immensely. To all my work allies over the years, thank you always.

5   BURN OFF THE STRESS

I look back at my first job and it's the slimmest I'd ever been, which was 100 per cent down to needing to run off the horrible energy that I'd soaked up during the day. When people say endorphins release stress, it's genuinely not a myth. I promise you, 30 minutes of exercise to work off the horrible treatment you've been subjected to will leave you walking on air – at least until 9 a.m. the next morning. Give different classes or kinds of exercise a go. You might want to run it off, box it off or even zen it off in yoga.

These are all anger management techniques for you to try, but ultimately it will get to the point where you've got to decide if there is the potential to change there, or whether you'll end up festering away in resentment and never truly being relieved. The only fairy-tale ending I can offer from my story is, although being told no one would take me seriously unless I held down a job for 12 months or longer (particularly as a recent graduate), I was offered three jobs with only 11 months' experience. Despite feeling like an empty shell by that time, I was able to put the last of my energy into showing why I was more than a punch-bag, and that I could go on to have a great career. Don't let anger hold you down; you don't owe it a single thing and it won't help you in the long run – trust me.

If I ever hear similar stories from close friends, I urge them to leave the situation if there's no hope of progress. We're talking about your mental health here – you and your future are the priority. Whether you've been working for two weeks, four months or just over a year, don't worry about how it reflects on you, worry about how much your confidence could erode if you stay a day longer. The vital thing is to make sure that other people's intimidation and lack of control don't affect your long-term goals or the courage you need to find another place to thrive.

> Top tip: Freelancers are often encouraged to save at least two months' salary to keep them going, but having a buffer if you're employed can also be a lifesaver if you find yourself in a rut with work and feel like you need to escape. Money is often the reason we stay in jobs for too long, even when we're being mistreated, but if you can save at least one month's pay, that will give you the ability to take some time to recoup.

ENVY IN YOURSELF

We looked at how social media is fuelling our addiction to trying to put forward our 'best lives' in Chapter 2, but the truth is even if you cut off social media altogether, you'd still find yourself comparing your own successes to others'. It's a basic human instinct, and in some cases it can be the driving factor in making positive changes in your life. After all, to compare is to review the similarities (or dissimilarities) between people or things, and this doesn't have to be a negative process – but, somehow, we always seem to dwell on the negatives.

How often have you said things like, 'How has she done that, we went to the same school and I was better than her, how has that happened?' or, 'Have you seen all the things she's doing. I'll never have a life like that – I could never do what she does.' But why do you say these things? Why do you resent someone else's success? And why do you focus on finding reasons why you'll never be able to do what they do? The common answer is usually envy, and I've identified three common types that hold us down:

1   <u>STRAIGHT-UP ENVY</u>

We've had all the same opportunities but you're doing better than I am and so I'm going critique you to make me feel better.

2   <u>RESENTMENT ENVY</u>

I haven't been given the same chances in life as that person and never will, so I'll never do as well as them.

3   <u>FANTASY ENVY</u>

That isn't even the life I want to live, but I'm jealous of the glossy things and lifestyles I see in others.

So which one are you, right now at this very moment? You can answer all three – I promise I won't judge.

One thing I will say is to monitor the time you spend suffering from 'fantasy envy'. Sure, it's great to daydream, but when you start obsessing over a *Love Island* contestant's fame since exiting the villa, remember that they spent eight weeks on a reality TV show baring all to the nation. So unless you plan to pack your bags and put in the time at Casa Amor, I'd pull yourself back into reality.

As we discussed early on, you always have to be asking yourself whether such comparisons are really relevant to the life you want to lead. Very often, they're not. In my eyes, we need to change the way we approach comparing ourselves with others – being less negative and more positive; approaching it less as critique and more as sourcing inspiration. When we look at famous inventors, boss bitches or wealthy CEOs, they 100 per cent learned from the experiences of others – and leveraged them for their own success.

You don't need to be that person who social media-bashes B-list celebs or ridicules people's success just because they're from a rich family, instead why not start unpicking what made them successful in the first place and choose who you 'idolise' by asking the following:

* Did they have overnight success or was it a long-term process?
* Is there something about their character that helped fast-track their presence?
* Can you spot a strategy that they've used?
* How do they treat people?
* What's their work ethic like?
* What do other people think about them?
* Has their achievement made them happy?
* How much time do they put into their role?

By doing this, you can begin to break down whether these people got a lucky (unattainable) break – or you just might identify some lessons to apply to your own aspirations. The more research you do, the more you'll discover that most people don't just walk into book deals and get immediate standing ovations; they've had to graft for it in ways that may not be hugely visible at first glance. We all approach things in different ways and have our own shit going on, so unless you know all the facts, stop wasting your time lusting after a life you don't know all the ins and outs of, and restore your energy with positive comparisons you can learn from.

Remember: being jealous of ex-romances has never helped anyone build a solid relationship, so being jealous of people succeeding is unlikely to supercharge your career.

ENVY IN OTHERS

It's one thing managing your own issues with comparison, but it's even harder when you're having to manage it in others. While your friends, family, co-workers and partners might genuinely be happy for your next promotion or project win, naturally it can lead to envy and critical comparisons on their part. For you, it's unfair: you've worked hard, you deserve to relish your success, and you hope that the people surrounding you are going to be ready to pop a bottle of Prosecco when you tell them the big news. But the reality is, for many people it only highlights the areas they feel they are lacking in. Some will offload in private to other people, but the ones who struggle with managing their emotions might pop that bubble of joy of yours as soon as they start the sentence 'I'm so happy for you, but it does make me realise I'm not ...' And, just like the *Friends* episode when Ross and Rachel kissed at Monica's engagement party, your mind is screeching, 'WHY ARE YOU TRYING TO STEAL MY THUNDER!' or 'WHY CAN'T YOU JUST BE HAPPY FOR ME ONE TIME!'

There are many ways to manage these situations that don't result in tears, intentionally spilled red wine or a long-term feud, so let's go over them:

HOW DID YOU DELIVER THE NEWS?

Without realising it, sometimes sharing your successes can feel like bragging – particularly if you're reeling off multiple great things going on in your life. Just like posting your work on social media, it's worth thinking about how you position the good news you're about to share. What did you overcome to reach this high? Could you focus on telling that side of the story rather than just the outcome?

I'll give you an example. I managed to negotiate more money for a public speaking gig by one very clever sentence. I told the client, 'I'd normally charge double this fee so I'd really appreciate an extra £100', and by positioning the message in this way, I actually got a higher day rate and made the client feel like they were getting a bargain. Anyway, rather than bolting into dinner with my friends and describing the many ways I'd spend the £750 I'd just secured, I led with how I did it. By sharing my technique with them, it left them feeling they'd gained something from the story for their own personal progress, and it didn't leave them bursting with resentment – they just congratulated me on my smart thinking.

WHAT'S GOING ON IN THEIR LIFE?

Has your friend lost a job? Broken up with a partner? Are they struggling with a difficult boss? If so, it's worth asking them how they're managing those situations to see if they're emotionally stable enough to support you. You might find that specific day isn't the right time to tell them you got a promotion, but in 24 hours they could be in a totally different headspace – ready to down tequila shots for you even though they hate tequila. Timing really is key, and you shouldn't risk missing out on deserved praise by bringing something up at the wrong time. If they're genuine people, they will be happy for you when the time is right; but if they're struggling, maybe focus on how you can help them feel more secure or overcome their issues. They'll be much more enthusiastic on behalf of a friend that prioritises their feelings, so just save that message as a draft and get ready to read it out with pride the next time you see them.

WHAT TYPE OF CHEERLEADER ARE THEY?

Different people are amazing at different things. Some co-workers will dance on the desks at the office party with you, but you wouldn't necessarily expect them to shower you with praise if it's a sign you're better than them at your job. Some mates are great with giving advice on how to manage difficult people, but not great at encouraging you to take a risky new job in a different industry. And some parents will tell all their friends about how well you're doing, but never tell *you* how proud they are of you – particularly if you call during *Emmerdale* or *Coronation Street*.

Use different people for different news. I have some friends that I can say any amazing news to and I know they will send selfless streams of excited emojis at any time of the day; and I have some people that won't acknowledge my successes until I see them in person and it's brought up in conversation. Both approaches are perfectly fine and help keep you grounded. The important thing for me is that I've recognised these traits in almost all of my peers, friends and family members, so I choose who I share my good news with depending on the content.

Really analyse the people in your life and how best they can support you. If you've got lots of friends who will pick you up after a messy break-up but don't champion your career successes, find people who will. You might have to find a new group of people entirely, who want to see you succeed, who will be excited for you when you need it, and who will put you forward for things because they see being connected to you as a benefit and not a threat. You don't need to cut anyone off, you just need to surround yourself with a range of people who give you the support and praise you deserve.

CONFIDENCE IN YOURSELF

A lot of people say that confidence starts within, but the truth is your surroundings have a huge impact on your confidence levels. Where you grew up, what grades you got, how your parents treated you and your siblings, whether you were invited to parties or asked out on dates, whether you found yourself complimented frequently or not noticed at all. You can't click your fingers and forget your past, and I definitely won't be telling you to ignore it – in fact, I'm going to tell you to do the opposite in order to break free.

Choose something you're not confident with, whether it be speaking in meetings, asking for more money, challenging seniors or anything else, and challenge yourself to do the 'five whys' exercise (a tool used for uncovering the root of a problem). Here are a couple of examples:

'I'M SCARED OF SHARING MY OPINIONS IN MEETINGS.' WHY?

1   Because I don't want to sound stupid if I say something wrong.

2   Because I don't want people to think I can't do my job properly.

3   Because I'm junior anyway and I already feel out of my depth.

4   Because everyone here is so talented.

5   Because they're older and they've been doing their jobs for so much longer than me.

'I'M SCARED TO ASK FOR MORE MONEY.' WHY?

1   Because I don't want to look cheeky.

2   Because I don't know how much other people get paid, and don't want to cost myself out of the job.

3   Because I really like the company and don't want to ruin the relationship.

4   Because I don't actually know how to have the conversation.

5   Because I don't know how much they actually value me.

You see, when we keep questioning why we feel the way we do, we'll start to unravel the insecurities holding us back. It's through this process that you can identify what you can and cannot change.

Let's take the first example. If you're nervous about voicing your opinion because you feel too junior in a senior environment, why not try sharing your thoughts after the meeting with one person (preferably someone you trust) instead? That way you don't risk the embarrassment of saying the wrong thing in front of a group of people but can get direct feedback on whether you're on the right track. You don't have to throw yourself in at the deep end until you're ready, so find someone you can bounce your ideas off privately, and gradually build your confidence ahead of the next opportunity. The truth is, if they've hired you, they see the potential in you – but they don't necessarily expect you to walk in and own the show.

A big tip from my personal experience: even as someone who is very vocal and loves voicing her opinions, there are often times when I sit in meetings and feel out of my depth – and rather than bolt in like a bull in a china shop, I wait and I listen. I watch other people share their responses, listen to the direction of the conversation and only interject when I'm truly confident in the comment I'm about to give. It's so easy to feel like you need to speak first, but actually the key is timing and knowing when best to land your point. It's better to be the person in the room who says one thing of impact than it is to come up with lots of empty statements.

Another bit of advice I'd give is to let people know the areas you don't feel as confident in. No, it's not weak, and nor is it detrimental to your reputation – if anything, it helps protect the way you are perceived, as people know what strengths of yours to pull on. If they don't know you hate presenting your work, how will they know that the reason you undersold an idea in a meeting is because you were petrified that people could see the sweat rolling off your upper lip and you were minutes away from an anxiety attack? I've read endless leadership books, and the one quality they always highlight is being vulnerable and letting people know your weaknesses. No CEO or creative director is good at everything; that's why they hire people to work around them. And by being open about your weak spots, it also forces you to address the issues sooner rather than later – which you will very much appreciate in 30 years' time.

There are some people who appear to have confidence in anything and everything, without seeming to put any practice in to get there. But when you actually observe these people, they do practise something: constantly putting them-selves out there with little to no experience, and praying it will pan out. Don't for one second think the most confident person in the room doesn't feel some level of fear; the difference is they use that buzz as energy to drive them.

As individuals, we are often scared of the things we don't try. From bungee jumping to eating insects, it's the things that are infrequent that scare us the most. Brené Brown – the Texan, TED-Talking power woman – talks about the fact that we need to get comfortable with being uncomfortable, and it's when we do that we will have the confidence to grow. It's okay not to be perfect in every-thing immediately (or ever), but that shouldn't ever hold you back from putting yourself out there because pretty much everyone in the world has insecurities; we all just differ in how we present them. Use the five whys game to figure out what's holding you back. In almost all cases it will be a matter of practising until you feel comfortable, and if that doesn't work you need to refer back to my 'Blag now, worry later' mantra.

IF YOU'RE AN[D] WAY TO REACHING Y[OUR] GOALS DOING WHAT [YOU] THEN IT DOESN'T REA[LLY] EVERYONE ELSE IS D[OING]

ZOE BAYLISS WONG, FINANCE DIRECTOR AT DEPOP

YOU'RE ON THE
R PERSONAL
OU'RE DOING,
LY MATTER WHAT
NG.

CONFIDENCE IN OTHERS

There's nothing more irritating, off-putting and deflating than overly confident people. It's not necessarily their fault (it's most likely the ego-stroking they received from their parents), but it doesn't help you when you're trying to do your best and yet all you feel is overwhelmed. On the flip side, their confidence could well be the result of genuine hard work and high performance, in which case they're completely entitled to own their self-confidence.

The important thing for you to figure out is why don't you like it? Why does it make you feel uncomfortable? Can you pinpoint what it is about their confidence that grates on you – and if so, what can you do to help manage it? Is it envy, disagreement, your lack of experience or skills? Does it stop you from doing your job properly? Understanding what drives your discomfort can help you to control your emotions and behaviour.

UNDERSTAND THEIR HISTORY

For many of us, we don't scratch past the standard co-worker small talk and ask people about their home life, their education, their work history or their biggest achievements and failures, so our opinions are formed only on what we see in the workplace. The reason this person might display high levels of confidence could be driven by something you don't experience in the day-to-day with them. They could have run 15 marathons or once been in a world-touring band. Sure, it might not be hugely relevant to the work you do with them, but it could paint a clearer picture of why they present themselves the way they do.

This is particularly important when dealing with confidence in younger people, as the societal tradition is to assume that age is a defining factor in levels of success – but actually, people are progressing quicker and doing more at younger ages all the time. Make sure your assessment of them is fair before you critique.

LOOK FOR THE BENEFITS

There is always going to be a place for confidence in teams and project situations, so rather than focus on the negative impact their confidence could be having on you, how could you work with them to utilise this skill? During pitches? Interviewing strangers? Negotiating money? How can their attitude and approach help improve relationships or team morale? Speak to them about what they feel most confident in, and see if you can use their skills.

Likewise, it's worth seeing where their weaknesses lie and if you can task them in those areas. You might have a different perspective on them when they're in a more vulnerable situation – and they might benefit from your support.

AWARENESS

As with a lot of issues that arise in the workplace, it could just be that overly confident people are completely oblivious of their presence and the impact it has on others. If their confidence starts to have a noticeable effect on your ability to perform your role or on the others around you, try the following:

* Ask for a private chat in which you explain the dynamics involved or areas in which you or your team members feel less confident, and politely encourage them to be aware of this when projecting their own opinions.

* Ask a third party to deliver the feedback if you can – whether it's your boss or HR manager. Voice your concerns to them so they can manage the situation sensitively.

LEARN FROM THEM

You might not want to hear this because you actually resent their level of confidence, but how can you learn to adopt a similar mindset? How do they present themselves positively, and what techniques could you apply to your own approach? The issue could be rooted in your own low confidence levels, so rather than demonise them for a skill you desperately want more of, how can you get advice from them?

Confidence is something that can either be so hard to help people find, or it can be so overwhelming you question your own ability in response. But again, it always comes down to how you want to manage it. You can let other people's innate sense of belief grind on you, or you can learn exactly how far you're willing to let your confidence take you (and hopefully stop before you become irritating!).

COMMUNICATION FOR YOURSELF

I'm surely not the first person to tell you that having strong communication skills helps in all aspects of life. It doesn't just help you professionally, it helps you get the right haircut at the salon, the right food in a restaurant and your favourite song played in a nightclub (if people request songs anymore?!). Knowing how to communicate your feelings and your ambitions to different people in the right way is crucial to how well you're liked and how far you will go.

Here's a checklist of people I'd take some inspo from when it comes to communication:

- ## BE MORE BARACK (CLEAR AND CONCISE WITH YOUR MESSAGE)

  Barack and Michelle Obama are such brilliant speakers because they get to the point and only use the exact amount of words that are needed. As British people, we tend to waffle Hugh Grant–style and overcomplicate a sentence with erms, maybes, ifs and a bunch of other things that didn't need to be said. Instead, GET TO THE POINT and get to it quickly. Make your message universally easy to understand and not reliant on the inner workings of your slightly scattered mind.

A good exercise is to write down the points you want to make as a long full sentence and challenge yourself to shorten it at least twice. See if you can land your message in a much more compact way that will stay in people's mind. You can also talk through your ideas with other people, and ask them if they understand your thinking and how they might suggest trimming down your message. Assertiveness helps people build a reputation as a good communicator and decision-maker, so try not to word-vomit and go off track – and practise in the mirror if you need to, or even record it if you're not keen on seeing your reflection!

• BE MORE GRETA THUNBERG (KNOW YOUR SHIT INSIDE OUT)

When you look at Greta Thunberg, she's a prime example that with knowledge comes power. She's so convincing precisely because she's done her homework and knows her facts. It's mesmerising that someone of her age has so much knowledge on an issue the mass audiences don't seem to know anything about, and she's been able to cut through global clutter to bring her opinions to the surface. As someone who likes to advocate winging it, even I can openly say that the more you know your subject, the more convincing your communication will be to others. To bullet-proof any ideas you have, try to always consider other people's perspective. Someone who understands the whole picture holds so much more power if they are ever questioned or challenged, and it helps to empathise with other people's views.

BE MORE DAVID LETTERMAN (ACTUALLY LISTEN TO PEOPLE)

If you've ever watched David Letterman on TV, you'll notice that the dialogue from the celebrity isn't driven by them – it's driven by Letterman's ability to listen and ask the right questions. Active listening – where you don't propose a response or a solution – is an incredible skill that is often overlooked.

It's something that the world definitely needs more of, but to do it properly you have to:

* Commit your full attention, with no distractions or preconceptions.
* Have an open attitude, removing your personal bias and emotions.
* Show you are listening via your body language, with responsive actions.
* Avoid judgement and ask questions.

BE MORE CHRISSY TEIGEN (MORE OPEN ABOUT WHO YOU ARE)

The perfectionists reading this book might struggle with this, but the more open you are, the more people understand your behaviours, emotions and beliefs. Whether it's to lighten the load of your own experience or to help inspire people who are going through something similar, allowing yourself to be open, like Chrissy Teigen, helps people empathise with you.

If you don't tell people you're struggling with mental health or a heavy workload, how will they know whether what they experience of you is representative of your true self? It's okay to say you're struggling or you have struggled and let people into your world, particularly if it might positively change their expectations of you.

• BE MORE ADELE (ACCESSIBLE AND RELATABLE)

Whether it's laughing at your own shit jokes or controlling your resting bitchface, using communication in a versatile way will help you to appear more approachable and accessible. When you watch Adele in interviews, you aren't just drawn to her cockney accent, you're drawn to her down-to-earth attitude. It isn't ever overbearing, it's honest – and it makes you feel like you've known her for years. And if you're a real diehard fan, you'll even remember that she also drunk-tweeted so much her management banned her from using her own Twitter account (and what's more relatable than that?!). Now, I'm not advising that you let alcohol take over your social media, but letting people see the different sides of you is something that helps build relationships.

A big factor in making yourself relatable is really knowing who is in the room – their beliefs, backgrounds, passions and challenges – and asking what you can call upon from your own life experience that might bridge the gap between you and them? If you're about to talk to children from low-income backgrounds about your career, what parallels can you draw even if you didn't have the same start in life? Or if you're trying to wow a room full of very well-established industry professionals, what's the most reputable thing about yourself you can communicate to put you on the same page?

• BE MORE STORMZY (DON'T GIVE UP EASILY)

After reading Stormzy's book *Rise Up* I felt even more empowered and impressed by his success, identifying that one of his best qualities (described by himself and others) is his perseverance. When he is told no he always questions *why* to find a new solution. When he's met with barriers he always questions *how* could we do it bigger and better. And when he sees that things aren't being done he questions *what* he could do to create change. Because his inquisitive nature is driven by his ambitions, he is never deemed as difficult or demanding. He's celebrated as a visionary. It's his hunger to do more that makes his perseverance a positive attribute and something we can all learn from when it comes to our own communications.

I genuinely believe that communication is the key to forming the best relationships possible with people, but also to help show the best representation of yourself. So give it a go: try to concentrate 10 per cent more on improving your communication style when talking about yourself and with others. I promise you won't be disappointed.

COMMUNICATION WITH OTHERS

I think we've all had those moments where you get an email from a boss, colleague, client or even partner and think, *Why on earth have you worded that message like that? Are they that stupid, immature, inconsiderate or unaware of my feelings?! I would never send something like that!* But as obvious as it is for you, it's often not obvious to them why it was so bad. You could take it as a personal dig or it could have a significant impact on team morale, but you really don't want to be the person creating that kind of bad vibe. As I've said many times before, you can't control how other people behave but you can control the way you respond.

So in these situations, all you can ever do is question why they may have communicated something in that way and what can you do to change it.

Things to consider from their perspective:

* How are they feeling personally? Are they going through something you might be unaware of?
* What are the work pressures from their bosses, the team around them and their workload?
* Has this behaviour happened before – if so, when? What was it about? Who was involved? How was it resolved?
* Is there anyone else involved? Is their involvement positive or negative?
* What are their personal goals, KPIs or measurements of success?
* Where are their areas of weakness in relation to the issue?

By considering all these aspects, you can start to pick out the important information and consider how you might articulate a solution or avoid a similar situation in the future. It's also worth considering how you communicate with them, and whether you need to make any improvements to your own dialogue. No matter where you work, you will always have to find solutions to working with people who don't share your values or vision, so it's important to keep an eye out for the following three profiles and embrace these steps to build a strong relationship:

- ## CONTRARY MARYS: THE BOSSES WHO DON'T ARTICULATE WHAT THEY REALLY WANT

  If you've never experienced this, lucky you! One of the hardest and most frustrating things is trying to manage upwards with bad communicators, particularly if they're the people who determine your pay rises. Even if it's not a boss, you're more than likely going to come across a colleague who doesn't brief you properly – which only ever ends in wasted hours and a blushing face when you're made to feel like you've completely missed the mark.

  There are usually two things which have led to the wrong end result: not enough time and a lack of clarity. It's very easy to misunderstand expectations when you've not been briefed properly, and more often than not it's because that person hasn't spent enough time making sure it's understood. So before you begin any piece of work, always insist on blocking out some time to get a proper briefing, and let people know your expectations of the session. Encourage them to give you a clear brief with exactly what they're looking for, and if they're underprepared make sure you ask them the following questions:

  * What does a good outcome look like for this?

* Have you got relevant work for me to use as a starting point?
* Who needs to review and approve the work?
* Is there anything I should avoid?
* What key information should I definitely include?
* Are we aware of anything this person specifically won't like?

A really good tip is to always try to set up an interim catch-up to make sure you're on the right track. I know that can be tricky if the turnaround is only a day, but there really is nothing worse than spending eight hours on something that gets thrown out two minutes before the deadline. Plus, it covers you in the case of characters who are known for changing direction at the last minute. Remember, don't let the Contrary Marys steal your confidence. The best way to position this setup meeting is by insisting it will improve effectiveness and efficiency. No one will want to argue with that.

PASSIVE-AGGRESSIVE PAMS: THE PEOPLE WHO DON'T GET TO THE POINT OF THE ISSUE BUT STILL MAKE IT AN ISSUE

Passive-aggressiveness causes that horrible feeling where someone has made you uncomfortable but you can't quite put your finger on why. It's the flatmates who make a joke about your two-day-old washing-up by the sink, rather than just asking you nicely to tidy up your plates because their friends are coming around. Or in a work scenario, it's the people who congratulate you on your work with 'You did your best'. It's those sly comments that aren't so outrageous that they don't comply with office politics, but are loaded enough to press your buttons.

They're the type of people who say:

* 'Fine, whatever'
* 'I didn't realise you were in a rush'
* 'If you really want to'
* 'If only everyone were as confident as you'
* 'I wouldn't have done it like that but ...'
* 'That's timely'
* 'Ohhhh, I thought you understood'
* 'I wouldn't have put you down for something like this'

You know – those people who want to make a point about something indirectly but it just ends up being catty.

Their behaviour could stem from a whole load of personal issues, but remember, you're usually not the cause – it's a personal problem they have. So, whatever you do, avoid lashing out and throwing a cheap shot back in retaliation. If they're doing it in front of people, you can guarantee the rest of the room will spot their behaviour without you blowing up and pointing it out. And if they're doing it privately, just kill them with kindness and don't give them the ammunition against you. The best thing you can do is document when this behaviour is popping up and what the reoccurring topics are so you can observe what might be the driving factor.

From experience, a good way to address the issue is to ask them questions (preferably in person) like:

* What makes you say that?
* Is everything okay? I've noticed you've joked about this a couple of times, so I just wanted to check if there was anything you wanted to chat about?

* Is there something you might have done differently?
* I hope I haven't offended you at all?

By calling out their comments with genuine questions, you position yourself as someone who is aware there is something causing an issue but that you're keen to find a solution. It makes them think twice about what they're saying to you, and if they can't give you a way to change the situation, then it's usually nothing to do with you – it really is just them.

As we've talked about a lot in this chapter regarding other communication issues, the solution often involves really focusing on what that person's frustrations may be to help bridge the gap and avoid future instances of passive-aggressiveness. Make it your mission to create a welcoming relationship in order to discuss what the barriers might be and see how you can strategise around them. If it's because you're a young manager looking after staff who are older, your focus needs to be on proving you have the experience to lead and earn respect. If it's a jealous co-worker who wants the work you get given, how can you include them so you're working together as opposed to competing? The bigger a person you can be, the more your reputation will continue to rise and your ability to manage these types of behaviours will shine through – think of it as character-building.

DEFENSIVE DEIRDRES: THE PEOPLE WHO SHUT DOWN YOUR SUGGESTIONS NO MATTER HOW GOOD THEY ARE

Someone being overly defensive for no explicable reason can be such a draining process for you to handle, and it's often the easiest to get wound up by. But one of the best tactics I've adopted for these types of characters is continuing to push past the initial few brick walls and creating a safe space for them so they feel you're either working as part of a team or you're not a threat to them.

People can feel defensive for a whole load of reasons, many of which we've mentioned before: feeling overtaken, feeling uninvolved, feeling like less of a priority, feeling like your ideas may be better than theirs, feeling like they've messed up and don't want to admit it ... But your role is to always find out more, and try to change the relationship so that instead of constantly shutting down, they start to open up.

There are three key things I'd encourage you to do that can help with this:

1   KEEP BEING SUPPORTIVE

Having a consistently positive and professional attitude towards defensive characters is key to making sure your reputation doesn't go down the drain like theirs might do. This can be done verbally, through clear and concise dialogue with one another, complimenting them when they've done a good job and supporting them even when you know you might not get the gratitude you deserve. It should go without saying that bitching about their behaviour publicly probably isn't the best idea; only make it known to the people who can help you overcome it. Treat defensive colleagues the same way you would appreciative ones, and show that you're a cooperative co-worker.

2   KEEP YOUR COOL (AND THEIRS!)

When you feel like you're constantly battling someone with a negative attitude, it can be really easy to mirror their bad habits – so try to keep a neutral tone of voice and control your body language wherever possible. Hold eye contact so they feel listened to, make your posture open, avoid folding your arms, and make sure you give them time to discuss their opinions because regular interruptions can often lead to further drama. You want to ensure that everything you do is creating a space where both opinions are valued. It's also worth assessing whether their actions could be driven by tiredness, stress or hunger (we all know what being hangry can do), and in those moments, opt for a break from the discussion. I've personally found going for walks with people helps to take them out of the constraints of an office space and allows them to cool down and have a calmer conversation.

3   KEEP IT CONSIDERATE

The best people in the room to manage these types of characters are the ones who have learned the skill of diplomacy. Being diplomatic is being able to communicate your opinion, knowing what to say and how to say it without hurting people's feelings. It's important that people don't feel attacked or deflated by your feedback, and this is usually achieved by being fair and building trust. Making people feel heard and constructively managing varying opinions helps you to build a rapport with them and to make sure that everyone feels considered. Ultimately, it's about thinking how *you'd* like to be responded to in a similar situation – particularly if it's in front of a group of people. The more diplomatic you can be, the more people will respect you for not taking sides but instead seeing the wider picture.

Now, I know this has been a longer chapter – but for me it feels like one of the most crucial topics to discuss, because like many of the soft skills we need to conquer, we're not really taught enough about emotional intelligence and its importance. The emotions that I've selected in this chapter are the ones that, when I see done well, can be a game changer for how people are perceived and how they grow as individuals. You can't be a good communicator without understanding how the people around you like to be communicated with; you can't adapt to new environments without having an open mind; and you can't defuse situations without really listening to what the issues are. Conquer managing your own emotions and managing the emotions of others, and you'll have no trouble maintaining a profile that people want to connect with.

I want you to be able to walk into a room and tell people just how great you are, but also understand how and when to do that.

That is having emotional intelligence.

SHANNON PETER

Beauty Director at *Stylist* Magazine

What's your top trick to be remembered for what you do; how do you position yourself in a unique way?

'At the beginning of a task, I think if this is how I would respond to it in five minutes, then that's probably everyone else's route one approach too, so I need to build on that and look at it from a completely different angle. I'll take a problem and try to turn it on its head, which I think helps me stand out in my line of work. I also read really widely; you don't have to think, "I'm working in beauty so I'll only read beauty". You need to be reading about politics, you need to be reading about what's going on in the world of science – don't limit yourself. I'm also constantly reading novels and finding ways I can draw parallels between what I'm doing and these things that are so far removed from my actual remit.'

How can people embrace the saying 'Blag now, worry later?'

'Don't lie and say you can speak French for a French-speaking role, but I think people think that things are beyond them. I have people who come in and say, "I've never written that type of feature before" or "I haven't done a shoot before", but I learned on the job myself – you just get thrown into it. I think people are so afraid that you've got to have ten years' worth of writing features under your belt to be able to say you're good at writing features, when actually just writing one – but writing it really, really well – counts as a certain level of experience. I do try to remind people whom I speak to or work with of that – don't let thinking you're not experienced enough put you off putting yourself forward for something. If you know you can do something, then go for it, and prove yourself right. I'm a massive believer that if someone comes to you with a problem, you shouldn't show fear, because if you show fear, they're unlikely to have confidence that you're going to deliver something that is worthy of solving that problem. You can find allies and people who can help you and are more experienced than you, or more senior than you who aren't necessarily your manager, and they can give you advice to reach your goals.'

How do you manage failures and how can other people learn to let go?
'I'm someone who finds it really hard to laugh at myself; I can laugh with someone at something they've done easily but for myself, if something goes wrong I like to pretend it didn't happen and hope no one ever speaks of it again. But it's been a massive learning curve for me to realise that it's okay to laugh at yourself, it's therapeutic and you can learn from it. If you tried to block out something that went wrong from your memory you can't learn from it, so remembering these things that go wrong will always serve you moving forward because you'll come up with an idea and say, what's the learning from the last time I did this.'

EIGHT

FAILURES MAKE YOU FUNNY

f you listen to any good leadership or business podcast, the first and most important thing they'll tell you to do is to reflect on your failures. But so often, our version of doing this is associated with discomfort and shame because we focus on wrongdoings only. Sure, you need to acknowledge where the issues lie, but for me, the best way of owning things that have gone wrong is to embrace them with humour in order to let go and learn. Many of us dwell solely on the problem – but what if we converted it into a humorous life lesson instead?

If I've learned anything in my life, it's that laughing at yourself and your failures makes you more relatable and less intimidating. From the embarrassing chat-up lines you drop at your local pub, to your nip slips at work parties, these are the stories that people cling onto that show you're only human. I remember starting my first day at a new company and letting slip that I don't eat vegetables (yes, I know, shameful) and that I forever mix up my sayings, and much to my surprise, my bosses' reactions were total relief. They said my interview responses were so polished that they were actually happy to hear I had a few cracks they could relate to. They might have come to regret saying that as I continued to offload my backlog of Stefisms, but if it taught me one thing, it's that people want to see the unpolished side too. Nobody wants to feel like they're competing or keeping up with some perfect persona you've built; people want to be let into your world and hear what you've been through in order to understand you fully.

So how do you make failures funny? Well, you learn from comedians.

Pretty much all comedians have built their career through a lifetime of painful experiences that they've managed to turn into funny stories. Let's take Russell Brand – not everyone's cup of tea maybe, but for all the controversial things he's said in his career, he did spend ten minutes of his 2019 stand-up rinsing himself and the stuff he'd said during a BBC interview. Sure, he might have needed a year to realise that what he said was bloody stupid, but he leveraged it in his routine and in doing so rebuilt some credibility by identifying his behaviour as pretty ridiculous.

Comedians turn their failures into entertainment, inspiration and stories to remember them by. You might not feel like doing it directly after, but by reflecting on some of the obscenities of a process you go through, you can find humorous aspects to turn into an anecdote. They say the best leaders don't hide their imperfections – so why do so many of us insist on disguising our own? Everyone admires people that don't take themselves too seriously; most importantly, because it shows others that it's totally normal to mess up from time to time.

David Litt, the former White House speechwriter, says that the first time he met Barack Obama he blacked out, and he can't remember anything he said after that. But despite the slightly embarrassing moment, he wrote speeches and jokes for the president for several years and stated in an interview that:

> Sometimes, the best way to get ahead is to put your worst foot forward. In a world where everyone feels pressure to be perfect, there's real value in admitting that you're only human. When you can laugh at your own mistakes and get other people to laugh at them too, that helps give you the confidence to move past them ... You need to leave room for humility. We all need to acknowledge that we're going to try our hardest, and, even so, we will sometimes come up short. Only humor lets you have both doubt and self-confidence simultaneously. And laughing at yourself takes the pressure off everyone around you, because, when we're kids, we think the world is run by these perfect grownups. But then we get older, and we learn the truth: There are no grownups. There's just us.

It's true, right? We used to look up and think we never wanted to make mistakes because grown-ups don't, but the reality is we're all constantly learning.

I want to keep this chapter short, but to make sure and to help you understand how to reflect on a dramatic incident or story and find the funny side, I've picked a handful of past shortcomings that I learned to laugh at in order to positively process them.

FAILURE #1: MISSPELLING MY OWN BRAND NAME ON MY MARKETING COMMS

In true Stef style, I like to take on everything myself – and although I have some transferable skills, I am admittedly terrible at proofreading my own work. Having hustled to get myself a stand at D&AD New Blood Festival (a three-day event in London that supports rising creative talent), I knew I had to spend money on some proper marketing materials, including business cards, flyers and posters. It was a pricey investment, but one I knew would be worth it as they would come to every event with me going forward. And as much as I tried to prep to get everything ready in advance, when you're working a full-time job you don't always have endless amounts of time to perfect your side-hustle tasks. Trust me, it's a struggle. But despite the juggling, when I got everything back from the printer's I was over the moon. The colours popped, the copy read well and it was the first physical manifestation of the brand, so everything felt a lot more real.

I spent hours setting up at the event, and as floods of people walked past the stand, taking my business cards and photographing my posters, I was so happy that I'd spent the money and managed to create artwork people actually wanted to photograph! It wasn't until a friend dropped by to visit two days in and asked where the asterisk was in 'F*ck Being Humble' that I realised I'd misspelled my own brand name on my posters. With only one more day of the festival to go, I just had to laugh at my lack of quality control and hope that more people didn't ask me that exact same question.

Was it embarrassing that I'd spent six years in advertising, proofreading brand copy for global clients, but couldn't spot this mistake with my own brand name (especially when it was 200 point size)? Of course it bloody was! But it didn't stop me from doing anything over those three days, and for the next 12 months I continued to use the same misspelled poster as a reminder that I won't – and can't – always get it right. I've proudly stood in front of that poster at all my events, and never let it be a reason to be ashamed just because I messed up. I could have got them reprinted, but I didn't want to forget it. It's like a tattoo – a permanent reminder of a temporary feeling.

What I've since laughed about and learned:

* Remember your own brand.
* Always have someone to proofread your posters and don't rely on your midnight mushy brain.
* Don't think you have to throw it away and start again; no one's going to dwell on it quite like you.

FAILURE #2: THINKING I COULD WALK INTO OFFICES IN NEW YORK UNANNOUNCED AND GET A JOB

Ever since living in the States when I was younger, I've always wanted to go back to New York and conquer the working world as an adult. But with even stricter immigration laws than there were 20 years ago, the chances of me scoring a visa are limited, and I've finally come to terms with that. The journey to get to this point of acceptance, however, was an unforgettable one.

A couple of years ago, a friend and I headed to New York for the purpose of sight-seeing, partying and blowing our Christmas bonuses, but while I was out there I thought I'd try my luck at getting a job through the (unsuccessful, as it turns out) means of walking into numerous dream companies' offices requesting impromptu interviews with senior people. I started at TED Talks, where I'd recently submitted an application, but as I confidently walked in I was stopped by security and told that unless I had a meeting, there was no way I was getting through the barriers.

As I sloped out feeling slightly rejected and a little lower on optimism, we walked past the address of Wieden+Kennedy New York, which was high on my hit list of dream advertising agencies to work for. With the emotional support of my friend, I picked myself up and plunged into the building – only this time, I bypassed security and walked straight into the lift. I said to myself I would get off at every floor until I found the Wieden+Kennedy office, but as the lift doors opened on the first floor it just so happened to be the right one.

I walked hesitantly into the main office, following somebody that clearly worked there; noticing me sheepishly walking in, he asked if I needed help and I gave him the 30-second 'I've travelled all the way from London' spiel. He looked at me quite shocked – as you would be on a Tuesday when a stranger approaches you and rambles on excessively – but rather than turning me away, he told me to head down to reception. If you've never seen their offices, picture a contemporary version of the *Titanic*'s staircase down the middle of the building, so as I waddled down the stairs towards Christelle on reception, I thought to myself: *This could be it!*

In a quintessentially British accent, I poured my pitch out to Christelle, a gleaming smile on my face and pearls of sweat rolling down my forehead. And her response was? 'If you haven't got an appointment, you're not seeing anyone.' I pleaded with her in so many different ways until she insisted I leave the building; and at the risk of being ushered out by security, I agreed it was time for me to go. I don't think I even waited to leave the building before I started laughing at myself about what I'd just done; I'd roamed around the office of one of the biggest ad agencies in the world, asking for an appointment with the MD, with no CV, no prior contact and absolutely nothing but a heavy dose of self-confidence. As I walked out, my friend looked so hopeful, thinking I'd smashed it and was coming down to tell her I'd landed the dream job; instead we ended up laughing nonstop at how ridiculous it was that I'd tried.

But the story doesn't stop there.

Through the power of my brilliant online stalking skills, I found the guy in the lift, whose name was Frank. He was actually the finance manager, and I thought if I didn't send one last message, I'd always kick myself.

So I sent him this:

> *Hey Frank, thanks for connecting. Unfortunately my mission to walk into a lift with you, turn up to your office and speak to someone about a job didn't work out yesterday! But you can't blame a girl for trying, right?! Particularly when she's travelled eight hours for the job – on this occasion the English accent just wasn't charming enough. But you were the friendliest person I met, so I wanted to say thanks for helping me not fall down the stairs. I also wanted to ask if there was anyone internally you could point me towards to connect with at your office? I'm an Account Manager at LOVE, previously I worked for TBWA and Liquid Branding and really I'm just dying to get my foot in the New York advertising door, which as you can imagine is never easy! I've been a huge fan of Wieden+Kennedy for a while now and travelling out here to try to get an appointment with you guys was the dream! Anyway if you know anyone I could speak with I'd really appreciate it. Thanks again, Stef.*

A week later I got this reply:

> *I knew it was a long shot when I saw you walking down the spiral staircase gracefully in heels unannounced, but I thought with that English accent you had a chance. Very ballsy move though. I personally loved it. Send me your resume. I'll forward it over to our recruiting manager.*

If you've read my LinkedIn profile you'll know that sadly the ballsy tactic didn't pull through, but just to receive a message back from him was almost enough. Enough for me to see that through a different – albeit slightly crazy – approach, I cut through to someone.

Now, I don't know the reason I didn't get a job – it could have been level experience, it could have been a busy period, it could be that I was branded as the loony who waltzed in unannounced pestering members of staff for meetings. But at least I know I did everything I could to put myself in a position to be noticed. The funny thing is, I don't look back on this thinking I wouldn't do it again; if anything, it just makes me think of how I'd have a stronger plan for next time I get past security.

(Frank, if you're reading this, thanks for entertaining me with a response; and Wieden+Kennedy, if you're reading this, I'd still love to work for you.)

What I've since laughed about and learned:

* Try to at least connect digitally with the person I'm trying to have a meeting with.
* Don't wait for permission when walking into buildings – just blag now, worry later.

* If you want something, find a unique way to approach it.
* Laugh about how ridiculous the idea was, not the fact that it failed.

FAILURE #3: GETTING A PROJECT SO WRONG THEY COULDN'T DECIDE WHETHER THE IDEA WAS GOOD OR NOT

During the three years of my Apprentice-style degree, we were forever encouraged to come up with new ideas for brands, then we'd strategise, design and pitch them to our course leaders. The competition between teams was on another level: a combination of *America's Next Top Model* and *I'm a Celebrity*...

Our presentations had to look beautifully designed, our ideas had to be perfectly articulated and we had to deliver flawless pitches with no cue cards. One project that will forever haunt me is an idea for London Fashion Week, because somehow during our creative development, we lost our way and went down a rabbit hole of thinking we'd absolutely nailed the brief. So much so that we did extra work to bring the idea to life – our presentation was overly branded and we even got T-shirts printed for the pitch. We were that sure we'd smashed it.

That was until we saw the reactions of our tutors. It was one of those moments where they said, 'We can't tell if your idea is any good or if you pitched it so slickly you've convinced us the idea was good.' Not quite the feedback we were looking for, and once we got our results back it confirmed we'd totally bombed it.

It didn't take us long after the presentation to realise we'd completely missed the mark, and the fact we'd made T-shirts to proudly promote our ideas made it all the funnier (and more tragic). Now, bearing in mind this presentation was in front of our peers, it was our second year and things were starting to count – we were totally mortified at the time. But once we soaked up what we'd actually done, we were in hysterics every time the project name was mentioned.

What I've since laughed about and learned:

* Make sure you nail the idea before you get the T-shirts printed.
* Being a good presenter helps cover up bad ideas.
* People will figure you out if your ideas aren't great – so try to make sure they're not shit.
* Avoid going down unnecessary rabbit holes by having regular check-ins.

WHAT YOUR FAILURES CAN TEACH YOU

You can't change the fact that these things will happen in life; all you can do is control how you interpret and respond to events. When I sit here thinking about the silver linings to a lot of my embarrassing stories, there are three key take-aways from learning to make light of things that have gone wrong ...

HIGHER RESILIENCE

Right from the start of my career, I've been put in situations where I've felt out of my depth; but by continually embracing these experiences and reflecting on them positively, my ability to bounce back from bad situations has been much quicker. I put myself forward for things I might never have dreamed of because I've learned to move on quickly and keep throwing myself in at the deep end.

With resilience will come a newfound self-confidence to either try something again in a new way or to try something even harder, knowing that you'll be able to find a solution (or, worst-case scenario, end up with a great anecdote). Having both resilience and unlimited self-confidence is everything you need to smash self-promotion.

IT'S OKAY TO LAUGH IT'S THERAPEUTIC AI FROM IT. REMEMBEI THAT GO WRONG WIL YOU TO MOVE FORWI

SHANNON PETER, BEAUTY DIRECTOR AT *STYLIST* MAGAZINE

T YOURSELF,
YOU CAN LEARN
NG THE THINGS
ALWAYS HELP
RD.

BECOMING MORE RELATABLE

If you've ever met someone really superior or even an icon, you'll know you can often feel intimidated and overwhelmed – but when those people have cracked a joke about messing up, I all of a sudden feel so much more at ease. The pedestal we put people on is usually built on top of funny failures, and when people share them with you, you feel like you can connect on a much more personal level. Barriers are broken down and you open the door for others to share and accept their mistakes too.

A great theme for posts on social media I've seen is #FuckeditFriday, a weekly opportunity to laugh at and celebrate messing up. Not only does it give you the chance to share your own stories; it also opens up a flood of similar tales from complete strangers who've done the same thing.

LETTING GO

I heard a really nice quote that should act as a reminder for when we're trying to shake off failures: Susan Sparks, TEDx speaker and comedian, says that 'If you can laugh at yourself, you can forgive yourself'. And I genuinely believe that. When you breeze over or struggle to revisit failures, it's often because you've not let yourself off for doing whatever you did. The only person that's going to hold you accountable or in constant regret is yourself. Although in your head a mistake might feel like the end of the world, you have to give yourself a break from trying to be this uber-perfect version of yourself and just let go of the tension.

When we laugh about things that go wrong, we get rid of the shame quicker.

Care less, laugh (and share) more.

MELISSA KITTY JARRAM

Artist and illustrator

———

What's one of your best attributes and how did you figure it out?

'I think one of my best attributes is being honest and not really caring about what other people think of me. When it comes down to it, the whole world is constantly judging you and inventing their impressions of you, and often they are really wrong and I don't like to waste energy trying to convince them otherwise. I think that as long as you know yourself really well (and this is a very important thing to do) then you will treat other people with the love that they deserve, as well as achieve your full potential, so I just focus on that and live my life true to my morals and work ethic. I actually figured this out when I was doing my GCSEs, and one of my friends gave me a lecture about how I was partying too much and was going to fail my exams, ruin my life, and not get into uni etc (which was apparently what everyone was talking about). After ignoring her advice, I got straight As and A*s ... and went to uni. Just because you're not doing things the same way that other people are, does not mean you're doing something wrong. When people judge you wrongly, the joke is very much on them. I guess that's the best advice I can give. Spend a lot of time on rational introspection, and get to know yourself.'

When was a time where you blagged your way through something and it paid off? How can people embrace the saying 'Blag now, worry later?'
'I was in Shanghai to host some art workshops and I ended up meeting an owner of a clothing company who was looking for a graphic designer. I told him that I could do the job, showed him my work, and he was interested and asked me to come into their office to start on Monday. He asked if I knew how to use Adobe Illustrator because that was essential for the role, and I said "Yes of course!"... Which was a massive blag. I was fluent in Photoshop, but never had to use Illustrator before. I figured I could learn over the weekend, which I did! Thanks to a VPN, I was able to spend the whole weekend watching YouTube tutorials about Illustrator, so I walked in on Monday and worked with them for a while. This was pretty important because it completely changed my own work. I only use Illustrator now, and it helped me to finally develop my own digital style.'

Getting the money you deserve can be tricky. What's the best money advice you could give to get what you're worth?
'My friend Sylvia gave me good advice about this. She said, "Know your worth", which is so true. Keep in mind the amount of thinking that goes into the work you produce, and

track how much time it takes for you to make it. You're creating something that hasn't ever existed before that's pretty wild. Also, talk to each other! Find out what your other freelance friends are charging and discuss it with them. Keep the prices high, but fair. I find that the big companies often pay well because they can afford to, and they're usually really good with that. It's the smaller companies that want you to work for a lot less than the work is worth, so I don't usually take on those projects unless it's something that I really support or want to do (like charities, for example).'

What advice would you give to people trying to overcome imposter syndrome?

'I've spent a lot of time analysing myself, and I know I have an extremely good work ethic because I often put myself through pain to achieve an end goal, so I always feel like my achievements were valid. I am also very aware of how lucky I am! I've had so many opportunities, so I'm grateful for all of those and to everybody who has helped me along the way. I suppose I don't carry any guilt for the opportunities I've been given because I know that I will help other people in the same way wherever I can. I'm actually quite amazed that people suffer from imposter syndrome, because how could you feel like you don't deserve something when you've sacrificed time and energy for an achievement? Everything that I've done has required either spending a lot of time alone (isolation, FOMO) and thought (focus), or staying up all night to finish something (probably because I slacked off to party/socialise), or feeling uncomfortable (long periods of solitude, sitting in the same place for hours, working a job I didn't enjoy in order to support myself when I was trying to get somewhere). As far as I'm concerned, if you've made sacrifices for your achievements, then you definitely deserve them.'

NINE

DON'T LET LABELS LIMIT YOU

Throughout this book, I've consistently told you the importance of self-reflection, but as I write this final chapter following eight months of having my head in a Google Docs sheet, I realise that I myself haven't quite processed how much of a whirlwind the past two years have been. I moved to London without a single contact to my name and knowing I had more to give – but I could never have anticipated what building this platform has done for the people around me, and most importantly, for myself.

No, this is not the part of the book where I pressure you to start up a side hustle or urge you to work yourself into the ground; instead, it is the time to acknowledge that we are more than our job titles. We have outgrown our labels of 'introvert' and 'extrovert'. We have changed the narratives we dreamed up when we were 16 and were trying to figure out our future careers. We are constantly growing, and with growth comes change – in who we are and what we are capable of – and we have to continuously recognise this.

Before moving to London, I had only ever been considered as an advertising account manager. I don't mean that in a self-deprecating way; I mean that I knew, deep down, that I hadn't reached my full potential or built the reputation I wanted to be recognised for. I knew that the 9-to-5s I'd been working all those years had been great for me in order to learn, but they hadn't taken advantage of everything I had to offer and I wasn't sure how quickly that would change.

I built F*ck Being Humble around the skills that I wanted to bring to life and that weren't being utilised in my full-time role. The public speaking, the event curation, the thought leadership; the breaking traditionally boring stereotypes down and finding a new way to talk about them. In doing this, I accelerated my profile in the industry, and at last I found myself being acknowledged for my own skills – not just as a cog in a machine.

Fast-forward to now, and I'm now being offered jobs where they don't ask to see my CV, for the first time in my career. Instead it's based on everything I'm doing with F*ck Being Humble alongside the previous content I produced in my full-time job. Maybe I shouldn't read too much into it, but I can't help but think all the investment into carving out my own voice and my own representation in the past few years has got me to this point.

Everything I've talked about in this book, I've done; I've lived it. I've spent the time rewriting, rewriting and rewriting my bios to make sure they don't include basic words. I've continually found ways to push through expected structures and find a distinctive voice for myself and my platform. I've regularly updated my website, LinkedIn and The Dots to show that my skills are growing. I've added £££ to my day rates and I've worked for free, which has opened doors I never thought I would. I've networked and formed some great relationships, and brushed off some bad ones. I've walked into event venues unannounced and got spaces for free with no business cards to legitimise me. I've blagged now and worried later when I said yes to writing a book proposal, knowing full well I am not a writer and I could completely bomb.

And, of course, I've experienced a bunch of failures that I've laughed at along the way.

I've sent tons of emails to speakers and venues who've ignored me. I've given out free tickets to my events to make sure the seats were full. I've had writer's block and self-doubt-hangover weekends. I've had unengaged, emotionless faces at workshops I've hosted and I've had people immediately dismiss F*ck Being Humble purely from hearing the name. But none of this has stopped the platform gaining momentum, nor how much energy I want to keep putting into my reputation. These aren't setbacks; they're unexpected directions that I had to pursue to get to this point.

But it's not just me I've seen grow. I've had:

* Someone stop me in Oliver Bonas the day after my event to say they'd scheduled a meeting with their boss for more money, and then moved on when they didn't get what they deserve.
* I've had an employee at Unilever say that using the exercises I've listed in this book got her a new job during their redundancy processes.
* I've watched attendees at my events stand up in a room full of 100 people and give unplanned two-minute pitches about their projects.
* I've watched people share side hustles that they were too scared to even start.
* I've sat on the sidelines being a hype girl during photoshoots as my best friends invest in real headshots.
* I've had a 50-year-old tell me that the tips given during my networking talk reminded her that she still has the charisma and go-getter attitude she had when she was a Club 18–30 holiday rep.
* I've seen my friend hand-deliver physical copies of his portfolio and get a call-up for an interview with his dream agency the same day.

I have watched the impact that these small steps of self-promotion can have on people's confidence and opportunities, and it's magical. When I talk about investing in yourself I genuinely don't think that needs to have a high numerical value attached to it (if at all); the point is, we can all cut through if we actually put aside the time to dream bigger.

What I want you to remember is, F*ck Being Humble is a mindset for you to adopt to make sure you seize the opportunities you deserve throughout your entire career. It's not about settling for the average; it's about listening to that voice that's saying, *Could I do more? Would I enjoy using my skills in other ways? Am I showing up in the best possible way?* It's about putting the skills you've spent years crafting to the forefront. It's about making sure you're celebrated for all the right reasons. And remember, self-promotion shouldn't be a dirty word. Care less, share more.

YOU CAN WAIT YOUR E[]
OPPORTUNITIES TO LAN[]
YOU CAN GO OUT AND C[]
THE WORST ADVICE I E[]
'STAY IN MY BOX'. NEV[]
YOU FROM GROWING, U[]
BEING THE BEST VERSI[]

STEFANIE SWORD-WILLIAMS, FOUNDER OF F*CK BEING HUMBLE

RE CAREER FOR

IN YOUR LAP, OR

ASE THEM YOURSELF.

R GOT WAS TO

LET PEOPLE STOP

SKILLING AND

OF YOURSELF.

READING LIST

Dare to Lead: Brave Work. Tough Conversations. Whole Hearts by Brené Brown

Talent Code: Greatness Isn't Born. It's Grown by Daniel Coyle

Never Eat Alone: And Other Secrets to Success, One Relationship at a Time by Keith Ferrazzi and Tahl Raz

The Confidence Kit: Your Bullsh*t-Free Guide to Owning Your Fear by Caroline Foran

The Multi-Hyphen Life: Work Less, Create More, and Design a Life That Works for You by Emma Gannon

Rebel Talent: Why it Pays to Break the Rules at Work and in Life by Francesca Gino

Outliers: The Story of Success by Malcolm Gladwell

Creative Confidence: Unleashing the Creative Potential Within Us All by David Kelley and Tom Kelley

Dream Manager: Achieve Results Beyond Your Dreams by Helping Your Employees Fulfill Theirs by Matthew Kelly

The Art of People: The 11 Simple People Skills That Will Get You Everything You Want by Dave Kerpen

*The Subtle Art of Not Giving a F*ck*: A Counterintuitive Approach to Living a Good Life by Mark Manson

Do Improvise: Less Push. More Pause. Better Results. A New Approach to Work (and Life) by Robert Poynton

The Emotionally Intelligent Office: 20 Key Emotional Skills for the Workplace by The School of Life

You Are A Badass: How to Stop Doubting Your Greatness and Start Living an Awesome Life by Jen Sincero

Start With Why: How Great Leaders Inspire Everyone To Take Action by Simon Sinek

Rise Up: The #Merky Story So Far by Stormzy

One Plus One Equals Three: A Masterclass in Creative Thinking by Dave Trott

Little Black Book: A Toolkit for Working Women by Otegha Uwagba